A Layman's Look at Life

A Road Less Traveled

Sean Ferguson

ISBN 979-8-89112-920-7 (Paperback)
ISBN 979-8-89112-921-4 (Digital)

Copyright © 2024 Sean Ferguson
All rights reserved
First Edition

All rights reserved. No part of this publication may be reproduced, distributed, or transmitted in any form or by any means, including photocopying, recording, or other electronic or mechanical methods without the prior written permission of the publisher. For permission requests, solicit the publisher via the address below.

Covenant Books
11661 Hwy 707
Murrells Inlet, SC 29576
www.covenantbooks.com

CONTENTS

Preface		v
Chapter 1:	Wait, How Did I Get Here?	1
Chapter 2:	Faith	3
Chapter 3:	Shot at and Missed, Spit at and Hit	6
Chapter 4:	Why Do Bad Things Happen to Good People?	12
Chapter 5:	Down the Rabbit Hole	18
Chapter 6:	The Bible	20
Chapter 7:	Science or Scripture?	25
Chapter 8:	Doctrine, Doctrine, Doctrine or Duck, Duck, Goose	30
Chapter 9:	The Devil Is in the Details	32
Chapter 10:	Is the Day of the Lord Approaching?	39
Chapter 11:	Awakening	44
Chapter 12:	Witnessing	53
Chapter 13:	What Is Philosophy?	62
Chapter 14:	What do I believe and why do I believe it?	65
Chapter 15:	The Big Search	77
Chapter 16:	Resentment and Forgiveness	81
Chapter 17:	Depression and Sin	85
Chapter 18:	The Big Promise	92
Chapter 19:	Wrapping Up	96
Afterword		99

PREFACE

I'm no scholar; I'm not claiming any special insight or authority, nor did I expect to write a book like this. This all started as a writing exercise to help me learn how to write. I thought I wanted to write a novel, but this subject has pushed itself to the front of my mind and won't go away until I write it. In fact, as I began, I wasn't even sure it would qualify as a book. How long is a book? How many words or pages? I'm not interested in filling space with words; I just want to record my thoughts in hopes that they will make sense and maybe even help someone.

    I never would have claimed to be a religious person until just recently. I always believed there was a God, and I believed Jesus lived, died on the cross, and rose from the dead. These are things learned by rote when I was a kid. I had a mental image of these things and had seen movies and many graphic representations of the stories I was told. However, I wasn't taught the Bible and didn't know that it told a complete story about mankind and God's plan for human beings. Despite that, I always found myself trying to reconcile the ideas of people who said there was no God and those who believe. I was looking for evidence in the material world to attach to the possibility/probability that God does exist. Decades before I ever heard the term *apologetics*, I was trying to be an apologist. So what follows is how this layman has come to explain what I believe and why I believe it. As I write these things, I ask God for inspiration and honesty, and by necessity, it is somewhat autobiographical.

    I hold some fairly strong beliefs in some areas, and my comments in those areas may appear harsh and even prejudicial. It is not my intention to insult or offend anyone. In fact, as I am a recovered alcoholic and suffer from clinical depression, I feel like I'm definitely not entitled to criticize or judge others. However, I have learned some things, which I hold onto for dear life because they have saved my life. I'm just trying to share some points of view I've developed over my life especially during the last forty years of recovery from alcoholism while discovering a new way of life.

This new way of life has got me stirred up and excited in a way that is totally unlike anything I've ever experienced. I feel like I have to share this good news with as many people as possible. In these modern times, I think many people are looking for instant gratification and personal validation. I feel like people want Instagram or some other mechanism to make them feel good. I hope that what I have to share will inspire or provoke the reader to look deeper in this direction for another way to find a real, dependable, and lasting way to feel good and secure in life.

What I'll say to you is please read the entire book. Take what you need or can use, and just leave the rest. If what I have written helps you in any way or even leads you to a belief in God and a reliance on the Bible, I've done what I've set out to do.

CHAPTER 1

Wait, How Did I Get Here?

When my wife retired and we moved to Chattanooga, Tennessee, we had committed to finding a church. Since I hadn't seriously attended church during the previous fifty-four years, I let her look for and recommend a church near us. As an aside, my wife had been fretting about where we would retire for two years prior to her retirement. While I was not a churchgoer, I was a spiritual person who believed wholeheartedly in God. (I believed in Jesus Christ too but didn't really understand how he came to fulfill ancient prophecy.) I told her not to worry because God would put us where he wanted us when the time came. He did! We live in a suburb of Chattanooga called Hixson. My wife was raised Methodist and found a Methodist church near us. When we arrived, we were invited to join a newly formed Sunday school class. This is where I learned about the fact that a majority of the prophecies in the Bible had already come to pass 100 percent accurately. *Wow!* I was blown away. I began to see the structure of the Bible and am learning more and more about how to understand it. I see the Bible as not only a story of how the entire universe came into existence, but it is also a Jewish history book. It's full of true stories and object lessons. It's full of prophecies fulfilled and the hope of prophecies yet to come. It illustrates God's infinite mercy and is sealed with Jesus giving his life on the cross to cover all our sins.

Finally, a reliable source! I wasn't taught this as a kid because I was raised Roman Catholic. I was in Catholic school through the fourth grade, and they taught catechism, not the Bible. Then when I was taken out of Catholic school and put in public school, my family became Christian Scientists. It's a strange religion, and we didn't totally buy into the idea of no doctors. That didn't make sense to our family. So I sat through the services but don't know if I got a lot out of it. After high school, I quit going to church until my first wife asked me to go to the First Baptist Church in Houston. I even got baptized again. I was inspired but not educated. We quit going after a couple of years when my wife started her own business, which required work six days a week. Sunday was her only day off, and she needed rest.

CHAPTER 2

Faith

Traditionally, both faith and reason have been considered sources of religious beliefs (Wikipedia).

According to Wikipedia, there are some ten thousand religions in the world. How do they know this? They say that 77 percent are made up of four main religions: Christian, Islam, Hinduism, and Buddhism. They don't even mention Judaism in this statistic. Possibly they don't consider Jews to be statistically significant. How strange since the entire Bible upon which the Christian religion is founded is a Jewish history book from beginning to end. Islam also shares its roots with Judaism. Fortunately, most other sources I checked did include Judaism as one of the top 5 religions in the world. The Jews may be small in number but are the foundational race in the Bible. This leads me to be very careful of the sources of information that I use.

So let's look at what Webster's has to say about *faith*, *reason*, and *source*.

Faith (in part)

1. allegiance to duty or a person
2. belief and trust in and loyalty to God
3. belief in the traditional doctrines of a religion
4. firm belief in something for which there is no proof

A LAYMAN'S LOOK AT LIFE

Reason (in part)

1. a statement offered in explanation or justification
2. a rational ground or motive
3. the thing that makes some fact intelligible
4. the power of comprehending, inferring, or thinking especially in orderly rational ways

Source (in part)

1. a generative force
2. a point of origin or procurement
3. one that supplies information
4. a firsthand document or primary reference work

So if you want to accept Wikipedia's point of view, faith and reason is the source of religion. Faith is a solid belief or trust in conclusions arrived at using philosophy or science. Philosophical ideas are a result of observation and speculation. Philosophers observe and examine the function and cause of things using reason and speculation. Science requires reason and rationality to make logical assumptions upon which the scientific method can be applied. However, science must first have faith in the methods applied to whatever it is they want to understand. That's interesting in so far as many people claim to use *reason* to debunk faith as just a superstitious construct of ignorant people. On the other hand, some people claim that using science or reason alone is a closed-minded way of ignoring the truth. The Latin root of the word *religion* means "to bind" or be held to something such as a belief. So can faith and reason be the source of religion when they seem to be at odds? They seem quite similar to me.

In looking at the word *source*, it seems to imply the origin or foundation of fact. A source is the point from which the knowledge of a thing is established. If a fact is established like gravity or 2×2=4, then we can have faith in that thing. However, it seems that if a source comes from a distant past and documents written in old languages using cultural contexts that we aren't familiar with, many people become unwilling to accept the source as valid. A good example is the Bible. It isn't 1 book but 66 books written by 39 or 40 different people over approximately a 1,500-year period on 3 different continents in 3 different languages and tells stories many find impossible to believe. Yet people can read books by scientists claiming the universe began as a singularity in a black hole, and they accept it as fact. Let's see what Webster's says about a singularity.

Singularity

1. a point at which the derivative of a given function of a complex variable does not exist but every neighborhood of which contains points for which the derivative does exist
2. a point or region of infinite mass density at which space and time are infinitely distorted by gravitational forces and which is held to be the final state of matter falling into a black hole

If you understood all that, bless your heart! It sounds like something science made up to explain something they don't fully understand and can only infer but not prove. But if you have sufficient faith in science, you can accept it, right? What was that about faith? Remember *faith* is a firm belief or complete trust in something for which there is no proof.

So exactly how is science different from religion? Written records from the hieroglyphics of the pyramids to the Dead Sea Scrolls to the Roman Empire records and many other histories have been proven to be reliable and are widely accepted by most scholars. Archeologists are constantly finding artifacts that prove the truth of many things written in the Bible.

I hope this will present a reasonable series of speculations on the ways Christianity and science can coexist since both require a great deal of faith.

Chapter 3

Shot at and Missed, Spit at and Hit

My early life was a mess, and I didn't have a life plan. I'm not proud of the way I lived and acted back then. I may even sound boastful or cavalier when telling my story, but nothing could be further from the truth. I guess at this point, I've just kept a little of my gallows humor. I'm now able to laugh at (not about) the stupid stuff I did and yet managed to survive.

In my carefree, irresponsible days of drinking and using recreational drugs, I had many misadventures and near-death experiences. I won't go into too many of them. It's called TMI for a reason. As an example, though, there was one occasion where a guy stole my .45 automatic from my apartment while a large party was going on by the pool just outside my apartment. I was letting people use my bathroom as were a few others who lived around the pool. Back in the '60s and '70s, it was common for huge parties to happen at different apartment complexes around Houston on weekends. You never knew all the people who would show up; it was just open to all. We would always ask, "Where's the party this weekend?" and this time it was where I lived. After I discovered my pistol was gone, I asked around and found out that the guy who took it was an ex-con junkie who owned a barber shop in another part of town. After giving it little thought, I went there late the next night and tried to kick the front door of the barbershop down. It wouldn't give, but it turned out he lived there, and I had awakened him. He opened the door, and I pushed in and grabbed him in a chokehold. I told him I was going to kill him if he didn't give me my gun back. He said he didn't take it, so I choked him until he passed out. When he came to, we repeated the process until about the fourth time he didn't wake up, and I actually had to revive him to make sure he wasn't dead. That's when he admitted he had stolen it but had sold it to his brother. I made him call his brother and arrange to get it back. The next day, I went back and retrieved the pistol. I won't go into all the things I told him would happen if I didn't get the gun back, but suffice it to say, I got it back.

Here's the God part in that. I didn't actually kill him even though I knew I could have and would have gotten away with it. God stepped in and prevented me from making the biggest mistake of my life.

Unfortunately, that wasn't the last time I had life-threatening encounters with others. One night, I was westbound on I-10 in Houston when I must have cut in front of someone. I didn't notice doing it, but the guy pulled up beside me shaking his fist and showing me the finger. So I rolled my window down and put three rounds from my .45 in the side of his car, and then he disappeared. But another guy in a big white Lincoln wearing a white suit and cowboy hat pulled up beside me flashing some kind of badge telling me to pull over. He must have thought he was Marvin Zindler (look him up if you don't know who I'm talking about). I flipped him off, hit the gas, and he followed. I got off at an exit in Spring Branch and cut down a dark street where some new houses were being built. I whipped into a cul-de-sac, stopped, cut my lights, got out with my gun, and hid behind a stack of building materials in the front yard of one of the houses. While waiting, I told myself, *If this guy comes down this street, he's not going home tonight.* I saw him stop at the entrance to the street and look for several long seconds. Luckily for both of us, he decided to drive on. Once again, I believe God was watching out for me. There were more incidents where I actually exchanged gunfire with others, but you get the point. Thank God no one was hit. These were the days when I didn't expect to live past thirty.

Back in my early twenties, I had started writing little poems or what I called Very Tales. I wrote them on bar napkins at the apartment complex I lived in. It was a big deal to live in an apartment complex that had a private (but not really private) club in those days. I was waxing poetic one day and wrote the following:

"In the Mirror"

In the face of death, I would be as brave or braver than any.
The thought of losing to it would almost be a relief.
Yet, I am sure that I would fight it fiercely, remembering,
perhaps, all there was to live for. Or would it only be instinct?
An instinct born of what?
Perhaps a selfish want for more of the living pleasures.
Though I have seen death close at hand many times,
I have never feared it. It is unreal.
Only pain is real and my fear of it.
If only I could face life as fearlessly as I face death...
But life is often painful; this, I fear.

I have kept that napkin for decades.

Back in those days, at the height of my drinking and running wild, I actually used to have two prayers I said. One before I went out for the night was, "Well, Lord, here I am and here I go." I guess I was putting myself in His hands without really putting a lot of thought into it since I never knew what might happen once I hit the streets. The other prayer was often when I got home, and it went like this: "Now I lay me down to sleep, I pray the Lord my soul to keep. If I should die before I wake, that would be a lucky break."

It wasn't until December 23, 1983, that I finally got sick and tired of being sick and tired, and gave up. I finally admitted I was an alcoholic and turned my life and will over to God in a new and intentional way. It was a couple of years after this that my first wife talked me into going to First Baptist Church because her friend from work was starting to go there. As I mentioned before, it only lasted a couple of years, but in that two-year period, I made my first profession of faith as an adult and was baptized. In Sunday school, we studied parts of the Bible, and the sermons were similar, but I never understood what the Bible as a whole was about. I never saw it as a long and complete history and never heard anything about prophecy as far as I can recall. Again, I was inspired but not educated.

It feels like I've been used and abused for much of my life in one way or another. I was sexually abused when I was five and again when I was eight. Luckily, I wasn't injured, but it was an experience I've carried around all my life.

I remember when my older brother had a paper route and wanted to enter a contest to win a trip to England. The two main requirements were that he had to sell twenty-five new subscriptions on his route and write an essay explaining why he wanted to go to England. My mom assigned me the task of going door-to-door soliciting the new subscribers, and I did it in short order. My brother wasn't that good of a salesman, I guess. My mom wrote the essay for my brother, and he won the trip. He never even thanked me for getting the new customers. In fact, it was viewed as my obligation to do it. A year later, he won a trip to Hawaii the same way. I sold the subscriptions, and Mom wrote the essay. He got the trip, and I got spit. I was only about ten years old at the time, and that set in motion a series of events in my life that were similar. I won't list too many but have some that I feel I need to share. They affected my self-esteem and caused me a lot of suppressed anger and resentment. They also probably contributed to my tendency to speak truth to power, causing me other problems.

Don't ask me why, but I worked for my brother three more times as an adult helping him build his businesses. The last one I helped build up to the point he was able to sell it for a few million dollars more than it was probably worth all while working for less money than he was paying less productive employees. Then he never paid me the bonus money he promised I would get after the sale.

I helped another company achieve a level of excellence such that one of my best customers bought them out for millions more than they were likely worth. That company had required me to sign a noncompete agreement just before the acquisition went through. My boss was extremely jealous of me and my successes in the company and used a flimsy technicality to get rid of me. Due to the non-compete agreement, I couldn't go to work for a competitor in the industry.

In another situation, I had invented and patented a valve for a particular severe industrial service application. The draftsman who worked for me and did the drawings of the original design tried to take credit for the design after I left the company. However, when he found out I was going to give my deposition prior to the sale of the company, he backed off his claim. I then assigned the rights to my brother because I felt I couldn't deal with the drama and stress and remain sober. It just wasn't worth giving up my serenity or sobriety for $42,000, and I was trying very hard at that point to stay sober.

I guess the point is that somehow my low self-esteem kept allowing me to get into these types of situations. By that, I mean I kept taking on these extremely difficult tasks by accepting jobs in troubled companies. I tended to accept any offer made because someone was choosing me. Wow, who, me? I think that may be part of the reason I have a tattoo of Don Quixote on my left calf and Diogenes on my right calf. I tilted at many windmills and spent a lot of time looking for an honest man. I think maybe selfish hopes and false expectations put me in unhealthy situations. Hindsight is so twenty-twenty.

Now, with God in my life in an entirely new and intentional way, I have found an honest man in the mirror. That's where it has to start. I can be bold without being aggressive. I can stand my ground better than ever. I don't have to have low self-esteem because I know I'm not perfect and don't have to be. I don't have to carry all these old resentments around like an albatross around my neck. I don't have to accept the judgment or opinions of others as defining me. I can lower my expectations of others and recognize that no one is perfect, and we're all just trying to get through life the best we can. I heard a guy in one of my AA meetings say, "We're not here to see through each other, we're here to see each other through." How cool is that? That reminds me of a scene from the movie *Oh, God!* where John Denver stops to answer a pay phone on a street corner, and it's God

(George Burns). He's complaining to God that he can't do whatever it is he's been asked to do without help. God says, "I've already given you everything you need." And John says something like, "What do you mean?" Then God answers by saying, "I gave you each other."

I've come to believe that we humans are hard-wired to help each other. I've found that if I approach another person and humbly ask for help, that person will almost always take a minute to at least try to help or respond in some way that shows a willingness to help. Some people may be curt and say, "Sorry I can't help," but in all fairness, they may be in the middle of something that they can't stop just then. But most often, I've seen people willing to go to some incredible lengths to help. It reminds me of a line from another movie called *Starman* when Jeff Bridges the alien says to Karen Allen, "I find that you humans are at your best when things are at their worst." That's how I like to see the world and its people because I believe it's true. The "milk of human kindness" is not limited to or defined by political parties, cultural considerations, or anything else. I believe it's hard-wired in all of us. However, we seem to put qualifiers on to whom and when we will pour out this kindness. I wish it wasn't so, but I am guilty as well.

So I've been shot at and missed, and spit at and hit. That's me, but by the grace of God, I'm still standing.

CHAPTER 4

WHY DO BAD THINGS HAPPEN TO GOOD PEOPLE?

I'm going to start with a question I've heard many times in my life and see where it goes from there.

"If there is a God, why does He let bad things happen to good people?"

This chapter is not intended to prove anything, but it's what I believe to be a reasonable answer to an old question people ask when challenging the existence of God. Through my studies and research, I have come to believe the following.

I believe that when God created man, He gave him a free will and a conscience to control it. Unfortunately, given the sinful nature of mankind, we see free will overpowering conscience all the time in order to satisfy selfish motives and desires.

Free will is boisterous, loud, unfeeling, uncaring, and often evil. The conscience, however, is quiet but persistent. It's always there in the background trying to get your attention.

In the absence of any governing law, free will can run amok and conscience can be drowned out. Yet the presence or absence of any law doesn't seem to deter willful behavior.

Not counting natural causes, which I'll come to later, we see the willful behavior of some people impacting the lives of other people.

Innocent bystanders are the people who fall prey to the willful actions of others. Some examples: a family wiped out in a head-on collision with a drunk driver who walks away without a scratch. The mass shootings involving innocent children. A plane crashes killing all aboard because someone didn't feel like doing proper maintenance or reporting on a known problem (like the Boeing 737 MAX).

The list of possible tragedies is nearly endless. What you will see in almost every case is that the willful actions of some person or persons were the root cause of the disaster. The drunk driver decided to drive drunk even though they knew the possible consequences. The deranged person who decides to shoot up a school full of children because his life isn't satisfactory. The list goes on and on.

Again, we ask why does God let these things happen?

I think, in part, that God wants us to see what mankind is like when they act contrary to His will. He allows us to make decisions based on self that are contrary to His will for us, and we have to suffer the consequences of those decisions. We presume to enact all sorts of human laws to protect ourselves, yet you can easily see how there is no way to cover every possible scenario. History shows us that regardless of how many laws we make, people are just going to break them anyway. If people can't or won't even follow the Ten Commandments and the Golden Rule, how can they be expected to follow thousands of other laws on top of that? Some laws are seemingly made just to enrich greedy and corrupt people, usually businessmen and politicians. I heard some say when you write a new law, you create a new crime. But many people want to blame God? Although He can be everywhere at any time to allow or prevent everything you can think of from happening, or not happening, God doesn't interfere. It's Satan running around the world, causing these things to happen. Satan was given power over the world when he fell from grace and was kicked out of heaven with all his minions. People want to blame God because Satan puts that in our heads to hide the fact that it's him, Satan, tempting mankind to act in selfish and harmful ways, just like in the Garden of Eden.

Regardless, many people use this false belief to claim that there is no God. Many people want to make demands of God but don't want to live the way God wants us to. However, God is not Santa Claus. Humans don't get to make a list of needs, wants, and wishes and expect God to provide whatever we demand. We must do our part. You know the old saying, "Pray for potatoes, but get a hoe." We also need to understand that God's will is superior to our wants. You've probably heard that God answers all our prayers, but sometimes the answer is *no*. Unlike Christmas, you can't just be good for a couple of months, make your Christmas list, and expect to get everything you want.

You've probably heard of *foxhole religion*, right? That's when the bullets are flying, and you've got your head down hoping you don't get hit. Well, it doesn't have to be actual bullets that make you hunker down and pray for help. I believe God wants us to think of Him every day, not just when we're in trouble. I believe every day is a day when we should take time out to count all our blessings and thank God for them. Even if your blessings seem few, you should think of all the things you have to be thankful for, and then thank God.

If you are a person who doesn't believe in God and you believe all of your blessings come from your own efforts, then count all your failures and shortcomings. Ask yourself how they came about. Ask yourself how you came by all your good fortune. Then ask yourself what you're going to do with all of it when you die. What comes next?

Some people are very religious and do all kinds of good work, but that's no shield against the misused will of others. I think if a person tries to live according to God's will, they will find themselves digging fewer foxholes. I think the wounds we suffer as a result of our own self-will backfiring or someone else's self-will running over us are the things people use to blame God. We could get honest and see how this is an opportunity to admit where we may have made a poor decision, which brought about some of our problems. It's an opportunity to exercise faith in God. We can say it's the fault of an unloving God, or there is no God, or take a chance and look in the mirror to see where we may have played a part in putting ourselves in harm's way. Nothing happens in a vacuum. If you would play detective, I think you will see that the one person always at the scene of the crime was you. How did you get there? Were you an innocent bystander or participant? I may not have always been the bomb, but I was often the burning fuse.

I am a Christian. I believe the Bible is a God-inspired history illustrating His will for us and showing us repeatedly what the high cost of self-will is. We are given a set of simple rules to live by but seem completely unable to follow them for any length of time. Why is that? If you read the Bible, it tells us that Adam and Eve were tempted by Satan to do what God told them not to do, but they decided to do it anyway. The price they paid was getting kicked out of the Garden of Eden and condemned to a life full of pain and hardship eventually ending in death. It changed everything God created for eternity. There were thorns, hard ground, precarious weather, and certain animals that became a threat to mankind. I believe that our sin nature has been passed down in Adam's DNA to all of mankind for us to be willful and disobedient to God. Just as the world was corrupted and changed, I believe that is just what happened to Adam's DNA. That's the only way I can understand the idea of original sin. Otherwise, I can't fathom how a newborn baby can possibly be guilty of any wrongdoing. It's simply a genetic predisposition to live by self-will. It is what is called our sin nature.

Don't forget Satan is in the world and continually challenges us to be disobedient to God. This is the great test of free will to see if we will obey God or follow Satan.

Many, in fact most, people on earth are not Christians and don't credit the Bible as being anything more than a book of philosophy, anecdotes, and maybe fairy tales. It's full of stories people have a hard time believing because they don't see anything like the miracles of old happening today. Faith is hard to come by in a world grown too dependent on science alone. There should be no division between religion and science. I think the unique characteristic of mankind is to search for an answer to the cause of everything. Science relies on faith as much or more than religion. They are both seeking the same thing but are taking different routes to get there. The big *there* is to understand whence we came to be, where we came from, and why we are here. Science looks at the mechanics while religion looks for the reason. Many people choose to live by their wits and compete with their fellows to get what they want out of life even if they step on the toes of others to get it. I believe this is the most common way bad things happen to good people.

There are miracles around us all the time, but people don't want to accept this fact, and they try to explain them away with science or vague nonsense like random chance. Random chance is a misuse of mathematics. Even the lottery with its extremely long odds is based on good math. Random chance is just a smoke screen hiding the possibility of God. Many people assume they need to take sides and choose science or religion. I think that's the wrong way to look at it. I was once asked if I believed in creation or evolution, and my answer was *yes*! I believe God created everything we see, know, or think we know, and that includes evolution. Yet much of what we believed about evolution is being scientifically debunked as we learn more. At the same time, nothing in the Bible is being scientifically debunked, quite the opposite in fact. Archeologists and other scientists are constantly finding new evidence to prove what was written in the Bible is true. Many people can't or won't accept miracles as real because then they would have to acknowledge a higher power in the universe whom I know is God. Miracles are not always repeatable and don't fit the scientific method. However, if you think about it, Jesus and His apostles performed many miracles many times over. He cleansed many lepers, made many blind able to see, cured many cripples, and raised several dead or healed an illness that would have resulted in death. That is pretty good repeatability, and it was witnessed and documented.

The Bible tells us to believe some pretty unbelievable stuff. It just doesn't fit with what we think we know about rational reality. The problem is that most people don't know enough about the Bible or science to make an informed and intelligent assessment. Both can be pretty hard to understand. Some people might laugh it off and call it the Force like *Star Wars*. They don't realize that's just a euphemism for God. Some want to talk about the possibility of *intelligent design*. They just can't bring themselves to say God. Some would rather believe in an ancient alien race that colonized the planet rather than admit there is a God. I think the reason is because if they accept that God exists and is real, then they would have to live by that set of rules I mentioned. They know they can't follow these rules, but they fail to understand that God knows about this flaw in us, and that's why He sent Jesus to be crucified and die to cover our sins. All we can do is confess and honestly repent while trying not to repeat the sins we all will inevitably commit. It's our nature to sin. All we can do is pray for relief from temptation and ask forgiveness when we fail. I believe if people could just realize and *personalize* an understanding of Jesus' sacrifice for us, we could find freedom from guilt and a pathway to peace.

CHAPTER 5

Down the Rabbit Hole

Here's an analogy I like to use. I claim that human beings are driven by a set of basic emotions. Like the colors of red, yellow, and blue being primary and with black and white being the extremes of all color, I believe humans are primarily driven by fear, pain, and hunger, with love and hate being the extreme overlaying emotions.

Walk into any paint store, and look at all the many colors you can choose from, and they are all made of just the five elemental colors I listed. I believe the same is true of emotions, and the combinations are nearly endless. Still, you can usually see the root cause (primary color) immediately. For example, a person might be driven by a fear of loss or not getting what they want or need. It could be a hunger for something out of reach or belonging to someone else. Of course, a situation, real or imagined, could be painful enough that a person could do all kinds of inappropriate things to escape. However, if you look, you will see what the primary motivating emotion is in any situation.

I am, by turns, gullible, skeptical, and, at times, even cynical. I'm basically a "show me" kind of guy. I have a scientific sort of mind, and I want to know the how and why about nearly everything.

When I'm not playing in my magical Walter Mitty mind where I get to run the world or be the man with all the answers, I have spent endless hours trying to figure out some of the great philosophical and religious questions of the world. What I finally recognized was that in my mind, I wanted to play God. I wanted the kind of power God has. Isn't that what Satan promised Adam and Eve in the garden? Didn't he convince them they could be equal to God and not die? He lied! The problem is that when I imagine this power, I don't really know what to do with it because the world is too complicated. I want to be magnanimous and wonderful and wise and fair. I want to punish evil and stop the bad guys of the world, but I can't even identify all of them because my point of view is flawed, and besides, who am I to judge? The level of deceit in the world is so great that it's hard to know who is truthful and who isn't.

Here's a theory I'd like to offer on why innocent babies are born with birth defects or why terrible or fatal illnesses occur. God created everything including DNA and everything else known and unknown to human science. I've come to believe that we have to go back to the fall in the Garden of Eden. The forbidden fruit from the Tree of the Knowledge of Good and Evil forever altered DNA in mankind. Man became mortal and possessed a new reality for reproduction. Adam and Eve have passed it down through all time. In his infinite wisdom and with a desire to have infinite variety, God created a recipe for DNA using four simple amino acids, AGCT. He made it so that there are nearly an infinite number of combinations that result in what we see when two complex sets of these amino acids recombine. If you look at a tree, it may be beautiful from several feet away. However, if you do a close inspection, you will see that not all the leaves on the tree are perfectly formed. Some leaves get eaten by insects, and occasionally some disease kills all or part of a tree. It's the same with humans and every other living thing on earth. The whole is still beautiful, just not perfect. This is the change God put on earth due to Adam and Eve defying His command. There is hard soil, thorns, and all sorts of things that make life difficult as God told Adam it would be. This is *not* the Garden of Eden anymore. Therefore, some things will come into being in an imperfect way, including humans.

What Christians have been praying for ever since Jesus lived is a return of Jesus and a new heaven and earth. Maybe another Garden of Eden and relief from all the hardships of this world. How about freedom from fear, pain, hunger, and hate? Won't that be nice? How about a new body that never gets sick or dies? Yes, please!

CHAPTER 6

The Bible

Many people don't consult the Bible or go to church partly because they don't trust what they're being told in church. Honestly, the reputation of religion is a mixed bag of good and bad. We see things like the Crusades and Spanish Inquisition and wonder where God is in all that. The answer is nowhere. It was Satan infecting the minds of powerful people driving these actions to grab money and power for themselves. We see others in positions of power and influence doing all kinds of evil while telling everybody else how to behave. These powerful people even make laws and set up traditions under the self-proclaimed authority of God or by the misuse of scripture to justify their actions. All the while they are doing anything they want without regard for how it may affect the lives of millions. So who do you trust? Trust the Bible!

Let me suggest this as a good starting point if you really want to get a good idea of what the Bible is all about. Download a Bible app, and there are several good ones in play. Most offer the Bible in many versions from King James to NIV, ESV, and many more. I like the NIV because I find that it's easier to read and understand while holding true to older versions. The app that I use offers many different lesson plans for teaching and inspiration. It also offers a yearlong plan called the Bible Project with extremely understandable animated explanations of each book of the Bible. These animations have helped me understand the proper context and who the people in the Bible are, their relationships, and why they are relevant in the Bible. The Bible Project is a nonprofit crowdfunded organization trying to get the biblical story accessible to the entire world.

To me, it makes the Bible more real. I'll mention other resources later on that have helped inform me and given me a better understanding of the Bible. I'll confess that I usually skip most of the genealogy because it's not really relevant to me. It's the way that Jews used to identify what tribes they belonged to and was very important to tribal people throughout ancient history. It also explains how the sons of Noah had many offspring and ultimately populated the four corners of the earth with many different races and languages (see the story of the tower of Babel). It was also a way to establish the fact the Jesus was a descendant in the line of David as predicted by prophecy.

There are naysayers who claim with absolute certainty that there is no God because they don't believe what the Bible says about the earth being created in six days, a virgin giving birth to a child, and that Jesus and others were raised from the dead. That's just common sense, isn't it? Besides, science doesn't support it. These naysayers don't want to believe in miracles because they claim that miracles are impossible. If they do witness something that is seemingly miraculous, they call it dumb luck or anything but a miracle. Even if they use the term *miracle*, they don't really credit God; it's just a word with no relationship to God. They don't accept the witness of hundreds or thousands of people from the first century and thousands of years before because the method of recording history was supposedly unreliable back then. *Really?* Word of mouth was the primary way of education and spreading the news back then when widespread written documentation was not easily circulated because there were no printing presses, TV, etc. However, when eyewitnesses from all around the region where Jesus lived and performed his miracles all tell the same stories you must believe they were true. They believed because they saw. What they saw was recorded in the Bible over a long period of time from many different sources, but the stories stayed the same. Oral history was reliable because it was repeated word for word over time with little variation. The eyewitness reports of many, along with the history written in the Gospels and Acts, have been supported by many other written histories from reliable sources. The essence and facts of every story have remained consistent over time. Even going back centuries to the time of Moses, there were thousands of eye witnesses and written accounts of what took place at that time, especially the exodus from Egypt. The discovery of the Dead Sea Scrolls shows that written records proving scripture existed long before modern scholars previously thought. The Old Testament or Torah has been copied word for word thousands of times in history. Centuries ago, in order to ensure each copy was exactly like the original, each copy was proofread by three different rabbis letter for letter. If even one letter or word was wrong, that copy was thrown away. The Old Testament is full of prophecies, which have come to pass exactly as predicted. I'll come back to that shortly.

Science is proving more and more that the Bible is true. Archeologists are finding so much proof of many of the stories that it is becoming harder for the naysayers to argue against the truth.

Mathematics is, to me, the purest and simplest form of scientific truth I can think of. Two and two are four, period, end of discussion. No amount of argument can change that fact. People can play all the games they want with it, but it will never change the truth. Scientists have proposed that mathematics is the only way we can ever expect to communicate with people from other planets (if there are any). I think God can be found at the root of mathematics.

So which ancient prophecies in the Bible have been proven to be true? Let's use Daniel as a good example because his prophetic interpretation of King Nebuchadnezzar's dream was spot on. (Jeremiah was around at about the same time and had predicted the exact period of time the Jews would be held as captives in Babylon—seventy years, exactly confirmed by accepted written history of the Babylonians and others.)

The king dreamed of a giant statue of a man with a head of gold, a chest of silver, hips and thighs of bronze, legs of iron, and feet of a mixture of clay and iron. Daniel's prophecy began to be fulfilled in his lifetime. Nebuchadnezzar's kingdom was Babylon, which was the head of gold. Babylon was used by God to destroy Israel and take the Jews into captivity as Babylon was the mightiest empire on earth at that time. Later, in Daniel's lifetime, Babylon fell to Persia (the chest of silver). Next, Persia fell to the Greeks (the hips and thighs of bronze), and finally the Greeks fell to Rome (the legs of iron). The feet of clay and iron have not come to pass yet because they represent a future alliance of nations of which some are strong like iron and some are weak like clay. However, the combination will be weak overall because of the clay. It won't hold together for long, and everything will come crashing down around it. When this will happen, no one knows. Many think it has something to do with a select group of nations currently in the European Union. Don't get hung up in some of the wild speculations people make about the end times. People have been making false claims for centuries. Remember, no one knows but the Father (God). The thing you need to focus on is the fact that so many prophecies from the Bible have already come to pass 100 percent accurately.

Back when Persia ruled, King Artaxerxes sent Nehemiah and some of the Jews back to Jerusalem to rebuild the city and temple, which had been destroyed by Babylon. Later, after Jesus' crucifixion, resurrection, and ascension into heaven, in AD 70, the Romans destroyed Jerusalem and the temple again for the final time and scattered the Jews all over the world, where they remained for almost two thousand years. Then after World War II and the Holocaust, Jews migrated back to the Holy Land in Israel, which was called Palestine at the time. By 1948, the United Nations granted Israel statehood and recognized them as an independent nation for the first time in nearly two thousand years. This was also prophesied in the Old Testament. It's a modern fact. It's documented, on film and in the flesh in Israel *today*. That alone was a major convincer for me. When you add in all the other prophecies that have come to pass 100 percent accurately, it's what the lawyers call a preponderance of evidence.

It's very interesting to remember that the 66 books of the Bible were written over a period of 1,500 years. They often repeat similar themes and prophecies of which many have come true 100 percent accurately. The rest are yet to come.

It is hard not to believe in the Bible when these facts are known. There is some hyperbole in the Bible and some things that may seem to contradict others, but the overall story is true even when told from different perspectives by different writers. I have seen many times people taking small quotes from the Bible to support false doctrine. If you go back and read the verses in the context they were written, they have a completely different meaning. Remember when Satan was trying to tempt Jesus in the wilderness, he, too, used scripture to test Jesus, but Jesus rebuked Satan with better scripture. All my life, I wasn't sure that everything in the Bible was true let alone 100 percent accurate. I had the same doubts many people have but have come to believe the Bible is true and inspired by God even if I still don't understand all of it. The preponderance of evidence is more compelling than some of the prevailing and popular arguments allow.

CHAPTER 7

SCIENCE OR SCRIPTURE?

The big bang still has no logical explanation. It is just a theory. Science says it began as a singularity in the center of a black hole. But where did the black hole come from in the first place? No one knows. It's just a fanciful theory somewhat like believing the earth must be flat because one can't see past the horizon. The fact that the earth was round was in the Bible centuries ago, as Isaiah 40:22 mentions, "He (God) who sits above the circle of the earth…" In the Middle Ages, scientists were killed or excommunicated for stating these facts in contradiction to the Roman Catholic church's superstitious pronouncements.

The universe *is* expanding, but that, too, was mentioned in the Bible again in Isaiah 40:22. Just because it can now be seen and measured doesn't make it truer than it was in the Bible. Science changes with new knowledge. Theories of evolution are constantly changing because science is discovering more about how it really works than how Darwin described it. Scientific theory changes as scientists search for new and better mathematic equations to unravel the mysteries of the universe. Yet the Bible never changes.

Who or what to believe? My answer used to be that I don't know.

How in the world is an average person supposed to know what to believe? I think I can believe what I see or lay my hands on. I know if I drop a piece of bread, it's going to hit the floor, peanut butter side down probably. That's gravity. I expect the light to come on when I flip the switch. But these are just mechanical things. What bugs most people is in their minds. Why am I here? What's my purpose? Where did I come from? What's going to happen tomorrow or when I die? We don't know, and we're usually too busy trying to make a living and just dealing with life to really dig into it. Even when we do, it can be too confusing, so we look to outside sources to help us along. But there's the rub. What source can you trust? Talking heads on TV or others who like to spread fear and doubt with bad science and urban legend? The Internet? Friends? Church? It was Denzel Washington who said, "If you don't read the newspaper you're uninformed. If you do read the newspaper you're misinformed." So who can you trust?

People who believe in evolution want you to believe that just because there is a huge similarity in body shape and DNA that man evolved from apes. But they can't find that missing link to prove it. They keep looking for the magical monkey that we supposedly sprang from. But that doesn't stop them from insisting that it's true. Even though the Bible has proven to be a reliable source of information for hundreds of years, nonbelievers still insist on scientific proof. The Bible is full of proof in the form of fulfilled prophecy and reliable eyewitness accounts. Just because things reported in the Bible are beyond the capability of science to reproduce or explain, some people refuse to believe. However, they continue to insist that their theories, which rely on vague or convoluted data must be correct. I call it large IQs trapped in small minds. So they say the answer is out there. We just haven't been able to observe it yet. If we can devise another piece of equipment or a new test or break the atom down into even smaller pieces, perhaps we will have all the answers. I've heard about science looking at the god particle (also known as the Higgs boson, which is actually invisible but supposedly detectable). What is that, and why do they call it the god particle? They're still working on it. The fact that they use the word *god* even if it is in a derisive manner still proves that they understand the concept of god, but they just don't have the truth in the way they want it. They can't prove or disprove the existence of God with math or any other scientific method, so they don't believe. It makes me think of the apes in the movie *2001* jumping up and down over a mysterious monolith. It's just too far out of reach to understand. Maybe that's not the best analogy, but it isn't completely off the mark either.

A Thought about the Big Bang

Since we can observe the fact that the cosmos is expanding as foretold in the Bible, I've spent a little time thinking about it and the concept of infinity.

What if the big bang was simply a tiny spark between two synapses in the mind of God? Why not? By definition, that would be a singularity. As to the black hole part, that's just a convenient construct/substitute of man to replace God in order to help explain what happened.

What's infinity? Some scientists have estimated that our cosmos is some twenty-eight billion light-years in diameter (some say more). But what's beyond that, another cosmos? How many more are there? Are they bigger than our cosmos? *Perhaps there be dragons.* We don't know, and it doesn't matter. My God is infinite. He always was and always will be. He is the master multitasker in that he can keep track of everyone and everything at the same time. He can pay as much or as little attention as he wants and to anything in his creation, which, I believe, goes beyond anything we can ever imagine. Infinity is unknowable; it's simply beyond human understanding.

Man is the only creature on earth that wants to know from whence he came. Some use the scientific method, and some rely on religion. The two seem to be on a path of convergence, and I wonder what that will look like. I think the Bible will prove to be the more complete, or at least simpler truth, not science.

The first thing I feel you should do is check the sources of your sources. If you see the Bible as the source, and the truth isn't stretched to fit some agenda that doesn't ring true, you're probably on the right track. I believe the truth shines in its own light. I believe we all have some powers of discernment. But it's best to do your own research too and ask God for guidance so you can know the truth when you see it. It's easy to get led astray by the increasingly feel-good doctrine of modern times. Some people call it liberal; others call it progressive. What it really is, is watering down of the Bible to fit modern secularism and rationalization of low morals. If you're willing to go to any length to understand the universe, why can't you make a reasonable effort to read and understand the Bible? It won't kill you. You just need an open mind and put aside any preconceived notions about it. Don't just read the Bible. Find a reliable source to explain it. Study other Christian books that break down the story. Read about prophecy and prophecy fulfilled. It's funny to me that so many people are willing to believe in the writings of Nostradamus and attach all kinds of historical events to what he wrote. However, if his writings were in the Bible, he would likely be completely ignored. Many, if not most, people just believe whatever they want to believe, especially if it makes them feel good.

I think that most people know in their hearts right from wrong. The idea of the Golden Rule has come from many different unconnected cultures throughout history. You know what things you wouldn't want happening to you, so you know you shouldn't do them unto others. Jesus even taught it.

Remember KISS? "Keep it simple, stupid." That's what I try to do. When in doubt, I return to the simplicity of the Bible. I know Jesus lived, died on the cross, was raised from the dead, and ascended into heaven. I believe it. The Bible is full of truth and teaching. Does what I'm hearing square with what I know? If it does, I bank it. Remember Jesus told the disciples that there would come many false prophets claiming to speak for God and even performing what looks like miracles. Beware! Measure what you hear against what you know. I don't know the whole Bible or even half of it, but I know enough to guide me through most of the traps Satan is laying in my path.

Remember, you can only get this base of knowledge against which to measure the truth from the Bible. If you can't or won't accept the Bible as true and reliable, then you're stuck in a leaky boat without a bailing bucket or a paddle. You won't be ready for the rapids and may be headed for the waterfall. Science is fine. It explains a lot of what we observe in the physical world but always seems to run into a wall when trying to fathom *the why*. It keeps digging a deeper and deeper hole looking for the infinite. Uh, please check the definition of *infinite*. You can't get there from here.

CHAPTER 8

DOCTRINE, DOCTRINE, DOCTRINE OR DUCK, DUCK, GOOSE

Doctrine (noun): a belief (or system of beliefs) accepted as authoritative by some group or school.

So is a belief any different than a theory? I had some tee shirts made that say "I used to Believe…but now I Know." Why? Because I used to believe blindly without investigation. As a result, I believed a lot of stuff that wasn't true or at best not accurate. Now I know with certainty that what I believe is true because I have found a trustworthy source to inform me. This may lead some people to label me as a religious nut or an ignorant fool. Not true! I love science and believe it has done incredible good for mankind. I don't believe it's all the truth out there to be had. Science involves too much unprovable theory, but don't tell the "science only" crowd it also relies heavily on *faith*.

Since the original disciples went out to spread the good news, there have been disagreements about doctrine, and it seems like dogma has become more important than facts.

Dogma (noun): a religious doctrine that is proclaimed as true without proof. More absolute than doctrine. Kind of like science at the advanced levels.

Why are there so many different churches in the Christian faith? Let's not even look at all the different religions in the world. Just trying to understand why there are so many Christian denominations makes my head hurt. Even within any given denomination, there are divisions over doctrine.

I think some people are looking for what makes them comfortable. Doctrine delivered with a sugar coating. It seems that many people fail to place principles before personalities.

Human nature (which is imperfect, willful, and sinful) can't seem to accept the simple truth and follow the path. We always want to throw in a few loopholes to ease the burden of following exactly Jesus' commands and teaching.

They don't call it the straight and narrow for nothing. Right living is not easy. It *is* a cross to bear. That's uncomfortable and nobody likes that.

Admitting our sins and bearing the guilt is painful. That primary emotional driver (pain) wants some balm to ease the pain. Maybe a little rationalization would help. Maybe I can measure my sins against someone who has done worse things than I have and therefore can feel better about myself. I have found that simply admitting my sins and asking forgiveness while trying to do better is the best balm possible. While I wouldn't want a list of my sins posted on a billboard, they no longer have the power over me they had when they were hidden. Secrets, with the associated guilt, will make you sick in spirit and in body.

I just ask God to help me separate the wheat from the chaff. Some churches don't seem to want to talk about the hard stuff like the book of Revelation and Daniel. Other churches only want to talk about the New Testament. The Bible is a whole and complete document. It must be read and studied in complete form for the story to be understood. So I run back to the Cross. I know I can't earn my way into heaven, and I am eternally grateful for my salvation through Christ Jesus. All I can do now is try to do better and ask for forgiveness when I fall short. I also try to learn more all the time while praying for guidance so I can avoid false doctrine or misinformation.

Chapter 9

The Devil Is in the Details

Perhaps you've heard it said that the Devil's greatest trick is convincing the world he doesn't exist. Many people have trouble believing there is a God, therefore, there must not be a devil. The many ways the Devil has been portrayed in art and literature over the centuries show him as a monster with horns, scaly skin, leathery wings, and a tail. Nobody wants to have an encounter with that, do they? It's easier to just say it's all just a fairy tale made up by religious leaders and used to control the masses.

> Religion is the opiate of the masses.
> —Karl Marx

I never liked the sound of that, but many people seem to believe it. That was just the Devil talking through a cynical and evil old man. There are many tools of Satan today infecting and brainwashing others to cause chaos in society. Evil is getting bolder. In fact, Lucifer was supposed to be the most beautiful of God's angels, and I think that's what makes him such a successful tempter of mankind.

> I have no special talent. I am only passionately curious.
> —Albert Einstein

That's me, passionately curious. I'm always trying to figure out the how and why of things. Before I began to finally study and understand the Bible, I vacillated between many different ideas and theories. I didn't have or know how to use a reliable source. I didn't trust church people for an explanation because of all the differing opinions I heard. It's uncanny how some people can pull select quotes from the Bible to support all kinds of nonsense ideas. Some of these ideas seem plausible, and others are obviously wrong. Remember, the Devil used scripture to tempt Jesus at the end of his forty-day fast in the wilderness. But Jesus wasn't fooled and rebuked the Devil with better scripture.

Now that I've found a mainstream Christian church and have learned more about the Bible and researched supporting information, my faith is no longer that which I learned by rote as a child. My faith is founded on solid ground with plenty of supporting evidence. It also seems like I've become more able to see what's true and what's not. Remember, *the truth shines in its own light.* I think you'll know it when you see or hear it if you're just willing to believe that the Bible is a real history book and contains teaching inspired by God. I know if you read the Bible with an open mind, you will see that it is about many weak and sinful people trying to live by self-will. You will see how many people in the Bible committed every sin you can imagine and how they suffered for it. You will also see how God's promise to never destroy man again as He did with the flood in Noah's day has been kept. Rather, you will see how he sent His only son down as the ultimate sacrificial Lamb to wash away all the sins of everyone who recognizes and claims Him as Lord and Savior.

I remember someone saying that if you believe in God, you have to believe in the Devil. Yeah, I believe in God. I'm not so sure how I feel about the Devil (that was me in denial). He's here on earth doing his evil deeds, and I would rather stay out of his way. My impressions of Satan were formed by being exposed early in life to Catholicism and Hollywood movies. For some reason, it sounded more unbelievable when I would hear people talk about the Devil than if they talked about God. There it is! The Devil is trying to get me to believe he doesn't exist! The Devil hopes I'll blame God for all the evil and disasters in the world. That's what a lot of people do because they would rather believe in an uncaring God than in Satan causing all the trouble in the world. Satan is like a serial killer running around without a clue as to who he is or where he is. It seems like, to me, if you mention the Devil or Satan, people think you're some kind of religious nut. Maybe Satan hopes I'll give up on God and just try to rely on myself. Um, that hasn't worked out too well in my lifetime. My self-will is not so smart. In fact, my best thinking got me a lifetime membership in Alcoholics Anonymous. I got more tuned in to God in AA than I ever did in church; that is, until I found my new church and got some real Bible instruction.

Speak of the Devil

Lucifer was one of the most beautiful angels in heaven, but he rebelled against God. He thought he could do a better job of running things and convinced about one-third of the other angels to join him in his rebellion. As a result, he was cast out of heaven along with his followers and was given this world to do his work in. His name is supposed to be legion. He is called Lucifer, Molek, Baal, Beelzebub, Satan, and many more. Sa'-tan, in Hebrew means "judge." Satan is always judging people and criticizing their sinfulness. He's trying to say to God, "Look what You made. It's not perfect, there are no righteous people." This is almost funny because it was Satan who deceived Eve in the Garden of Eden and filled the world with sin. Satan is always lying and trying to shift the blame to others. He's like an arsonist who sets a fire and then comes back to watch it burn while shaking his head and asking why God let such a terrible thing happen.

So the Bible tells us God gave Job to Satan to do to him every evil short of murder to see if he would curse God. Job didn't curse God, but he did contend with Him and defended himself to God. He asked why God was judging him so harshly. But it wasn't really God; it was Satan. Satan likes to have us believe God is responsible for every evil or bad thing that happens in the world. But He's *not!* Job even had three friends trying to get him to admit whatever sins he must have committed to cause all the misfortune that had come to him. His wife tried to get him to curse God, but he wouldn't. He wouldn't budge, and he never cursed or blamed God.

We seem to be constantly at war or about to be at war. Does that remind you of anything Jesus said about wars and rumors of war? Satan is very good at deceiving mankind. He can twist the truth including scripture to cause mankind to stray from the path God set for us. He would have us believe evil is good and good is evil. His lies are becoming more blatant and are being exposed regularly on TV, especially in the news. Euphemisms have become one of his favorite tools in recent years. If you call a pedophile a "youth-attracted person," is that supposed to make what they do okay? Political correctness is the same thing, except it has the added dimension of making people feel that perfectly good words are no longer acceptable, and if you use them, there is something wrong with you. Satan has infected many people in positions of power and influence. They worship the false idols of money and power. You could even say they've sold their souls to the Devil. These people in power, along with a loud and virulent minority, are trying to force-feed evil agendas on all of us, and we are caving in to these ridiculous demands just so we can continue to live comfortably.

> Those who would give up essential Liberty, to purchase a little temporary Safety, deserve neither Liberty nor Safety.
> —Benjamin Franklin

When this was written in the 1750s, it had a different meaning in the context of the time. However, it has been used as a warning for many years in its apparent literal sense to warn against any number of compromises that would have us surrender small and large freedoms to the demands of an oppressive government and an increasingly evil minority. Today, our government is overloaded with loud and evil special interest groups that are demanding we accept every wrong and sinful idea they come up with. Satan is hard at work in this arena and seems to be winning. Church attendance is way down, and the number of people who identify as Christians seems to be shrinking. Many in our younger generations seem to be totally self-absorbed and ignorant about God and the Bible. Many people don't identify as Christians; rather, they say they are spiritual. They think because they are basically good that they don't need to worry about the hereafter. They think they will be okay. But the Bible tells us that if we don't proclaim Jesus, he won't claim us as His and we won't go to heaven.

The Ever-Present Voice

Have you ever had strange thoughts come into your head, thoughts you don't like or want? Of course, you have. We all have. Perhaps these thoughts are about bad things that could happen to you or someone you love or worst-case scenarios involving a situation you're dealing with. Then there are the sexually oriented thoughts many, if not all, of us have. They are often brought on by looking at attractive people or seeing them in TV commercials, magazines, etc. Of course, movies have been providing much more than brief glimpses of these attractive actors. They show them in all kinds of sexually explicit situations. It's the kind of stuff we may replay in our heads where we can insert ourselves in one of the starring roles. We can even manipulate the script to fit our own desires. This can be a slippery slope, and it can produce a lot of guilt feelings. Yet we do it anyway, thinking it doesn't reflect on us, nobody knows what we're thinking, we're not hurting anybody, right? If that's true, why do we feel guilty? Perhaps we're hurting ourselves. Of course, we are!

Jesus said in *Matthew 5:28 that anyone who looks at a woman with lust has already committed adultery in their heart.* We're told from an early age that certain things are forbidden. Certain body parts are to be hidden. We don't comfortably talk about certain things having to do with bodily functions. The list goes on. I think about Adam and Eve in the garden hiding from God when He came looking for them. They said they were ashamed because they were naked. God asked them who told them they were naked. He knew right then they had broken His command not to eat the fruit from the Tree of the Knowledge of Good and Evil. This original sin is the foundation

THE DEVIL IS IN THE DETAILS

from which shame and guilt arise. Sex is God-given and therefore good. However, our curiosity and self-will compel us to satisfy our natural desires in all kinds of ways that can often be harmful to others and an affront to God.

Many of us are exposed to sex in various ways at different ages. I was sexually abused for the first time at the age of five and again when I was eight. I was told it was a big secret for special friends. Fortunately, I wasn't injured, but I participated just by going along. I didn't like it, and it affected the rest of my life. I carried the guilt of participating. I was curious, and I think I knew at the time it was wrong because it was a secret that couldn't be talked about. There was also a betrayal involved, and it made me angry too. I have carried this anger and the associated trust issues deep inside to this very day.

Sex isn't the only thing that we stash in our secret box of thoughts. Every sin known to man is likely to gain entrance to our thinking at various times. Anger and resentment will help us hold onto and even magnify these thoughts. We hold some of them so long, they become second nature. When we find our way to Jesus and start trying to clean out some of these thoughts, we may find it particularly hard to do because we've had them so long, we seem to depend on them. This is especially true of resentments. We can and should ask for Jesus' help in cleaning house and getting rid of resentments. The word *resentment* comes from the Latin *sentire*, which means "to feel." Resentment means to refeel something. We need to try and leave the past in the past. We can't forget but need to unhook the feeling that goes with the memory. We know we're not perfect, but we can't use that as an excuse for not trying. Satan is constantly throwing more thoughts at us and bringing back our greatest hits. I know about spiritual armor but find it hard to keep it on all the time. I like to think I'm building a storm door to my mind to keep Satan out. So far, it feels like it's more of a screen door. It seems like sometimes I even lay out the welcome mat. I'm glad to know that this is a process not an event, and I know Jesus knows me better than I do. Who am I that he gave His life to save my soul? It boggles my mind. Thankfully, I know that whatever I can't do no matter how much I try, Jesus will do the rest and then some.

Keeping this in mind gives me a great feeling of peace and serenity. Everything is alright already. Unease and stress are a result of witnessing all the troubles in the world. Unease is the fear, uncertainty, and doubt part. Many diseases result from stress. Stress alone can cause many physical ailments. The thing Satan keeps hidden is his part in causing all the troubles in the first place. He wants us to believe it's because there is no God or that God is uncaring and vengeful. He's lying, always! He thrives on fear, uncertainty, and doubt. This is almost a perfect description of politicians. They claim to have the answers to all the problems, but actually, they cause all the problems. Sorry, I couldn't resist poking politicians.

CHAPTER 10

Is the Day of the Lord Approaching?

Thank God we have a way out. The Bible shows the end from the beginning. It tells us what has happened in the past and what will happen in the future. In the Old Testament, the Jews believed there would be a Messiah in the future, but they didn't know when. Their self-will and rebellion against God cost them greatly throughout their entire history. They wouldn't accept Jesus because He didn't live up to their expectations. They expected a great warrior to come and assemble an army to destroy the Romans and bring peace and freedom back to Israel. Instead, Jesus reminded them of what was right in the eyes of God. He spent time with the lowly people and outcasts. He was the perfect servant. He showed love and provided healing but demanded nothing in return. He threatened the temple power base and condemned their corrupt practices in the temple. His miracles frightened them, so they conspired to kill Him. They didn't even recognize that they were fulfilling the most important prophesy up to that time. They were so wrapped up in their self-will (driven by the primary human emotions I mentioned in chapter 2). Fear, pain, and hunger overlaid with hate drove them to crucify Jesus. They refused to believe He rose from the dead even though He spent many days among His disciples and others. Too many people saw Jesus after He was crucified for the reports to be untrue, but they still wouldn't believe—or worse, they knew it was true but wanted to cover it up with lies. So they continued to pursue and persecute Jesus' disciples.

They were hoping to stamp out the Christian movement before it could get a good foothold among the people. This is where Saul of Tarsus comes in. He was a highly trained Jewish lawyer and scholar and became a key figure in persecuting the Jews who were turning to Jesus. That is until he got a letter authorizing him to arrest and bring Jewish believers in Damascus back to Jerusalem for punishment. But God struck Saul blind on the road to Damascus and told him he was to go and spread the good news about Jesus to all people, especially the Gentiles. His name was changed to Paul, and he founded many churches throughout the Middle East.

The ever-stiff-necked Jews simply will not accept that what was reported about the resurrection of Jesus was true, because if it was true, they would have to admit they were wrong about Jesus and that they had misinterpreted the prophecies about the Messiah.

Here's the funny part: when Jesus returns for the second time, He will come with the flaming sword, but it won't be to defeat Rome as the Jews expected, but Satan and all the evil in the world. Won't the Jews be shocked to see that it's Jesus come to the rescue? The one they so adamantly refused to believe in is the one who will be bringing a new heaven and earth and a new Jerusalem.

So is the day of the Lord approaching? Well, of course, it's always approaching, but when? That's what we believers want to know. We're always trying to read the signs of the times to see if they fit with prophecy. Yet no one knows the time except the Father, not even Jesus. We look for signs of the fulfillment of prophecy in things like Israel becoming a nation in a single day on May 14, 1948. Some call that a super sign. A few years ago, the USA moved the US Embassy to Jerusalem, which is considered to be another sign because America is recognizing Jerusalem as the capital of Israel even though it is claimed by three major religious groups.

I've come to discount wars and rumors of wars because they have been constant my whole life. They are just a byproduct of human nature. I hear people trying to make signs of many aspects of modern society, and to some degree, I guess they're right, but does that really point more clearly to the end times or apocalypse as many people call it? I think the one thing of great importance is whether or not everyone on earth has had a chance to hear about Jesus and make a decision about giving themselves to Him. Modern evangelism and mass communication via TV, movies, and the Internet along with the Bible being printed in nearly every language on earth have brought us close to complete saturation of the world. But is that enough? Have we done a good enough job of spreading the Word? I don't know but do know there are a lot of things stacking up that seem to align with prophesy and that it feels like we're getting closer to the end times. I remember reading something saying it would happen within the generation that saw Israel become a nation again. Do I have that right? Is it true, and what does it mean? How long is a generation? Does it mean the life span of a person born on May 14, 1948? People have been making bad guesses about this for centuries, and of course, we still don't know. I personally hope it happens in my lifetime just so I can see it happen. I'd like to hear the shout and the trumpet sound and perhaps see the dead pop out of the ground before I join them. Yes, I do plan to be in that number when the saints go marching in (big smile included here).

I have to ask myself if wanting to be alive when the Rapture comes is because I just want to see it, or is my flawed human nature wanting more proof of what I already believe. I try to examine my thinking a lot more closely than I used to because I know how much junk Satan throws at me.

I'm ready for the Rapture, I think.

The word *rapture* does not appear in the Bible. It evolved from Greek (*harpazo*, meaning to be caught up) to Latin (*rapturo*) to English (*rapture*). The point is I hope I'm ready for the Rapture. The Rapture is when Christ comes back and takes every Christian that is still on this earth and resurrects all of those believers who have died and takes them to heaven with Him. In 1 Thessalonians 5:1–8, Paul states that the Lord's return will be like a thief in the night, and no one knows the date or time. What I mean is that even though I am intellectually convinced of my salvation in Christ Jesus, I can't help feeling unworthy. I keep thinking, *I hope it's real and that even I get to go to heaven.* It's the burden of my past and perhaps my Catholic childhood that makes me feel this way, but that doesn't make it any less disconcerting. That's probably Satan in my head having fun at my expense. In any case, I kind of wish the Rapture would happen soon. I do believe in God, and I do trust the Bible. It just seems like my human brain slips a gear sometimes and my old thinking returns. That's where prayer and faith have to take over as a shield against fear, uncertainty, and doubt.

I have never been too firmly tethered to this world anyway. I've always felt apart from it, like an observer perhaps. I definitely marched to the beat of my own drum. I never sought success the way some do. I went for money only so I would have enough to do whatever I wanted to do. I don't mean the fantasy stuff like private jets, sports cars, etc. Just enough to be independent. I never kept a job for long because I couldn't stand the lies corporations tell or the way corporate culture works. I tended to speak truth to power too often, and I didn't care about the fallout. I have no bragging rights to a brilliant career with great success, and I can live with that. I just don't care about all that. Success alone is no measure of a man. It's nice, and I have often wished I had done more with my life, but I was unwilling to play the game.

An Inspired Thought about Dogs

This may not make a lot of sense to many people, but I think dog lovers will get it. I say it all the time, "I think two of God's greatest gifts to mankind are horses and dogs." Horses for the transportation and work they perform as well as their intelligence and loyalty. Dogs provide unconditional love, loyalty, and are nonjudgmental. They provide comfort, solace, and even security. They will even lay down their life for their owner.

In fairness to all God's creatures, I will say that I love most animals more than most people. Animals are not inherently sinful or evil. In my view, people are the only source of evil in the world. Of course, Satan has a lot to do with that, but we humans have been his instruments since the Garden of Eden.

So what about dogs? I got to thinking about how much our dogs adore us. They only want to please us, they almost seem to worship us. They depend on us for everything from food and shelter to health care, love, and entertainment. We are their safe haven. Yet they will still chew a shoe, pee in the house, mess up the blankets on the bed, and all sorts of little aggravating things. Sometimes we laugh, we think it's cute or funny, but sometimes they make us mad especially if they destroy something we value. We may scold them or give them a little swat with a magazine, but when they slink away with their tail between their legs and a guilty look on their face, we usually offer immediate forgiveness and love. We forgive and love them no matter what.

How much more does God forgive and love us when we sin and do things that are hurtful to Him? I wonder if God put dogs on earth as some kind of reminder or demonstration of His love for us. I wonder if God looks at us with the same love and forgiveness as we do when dealing with our dogs. I'm convinced He does. That blows my mind. I think it's a little more complicated in that we not only know when we've sinned, but we have to show remorse and ask forgiveness. I guess that's a little like tucking our tail between our legs and slinking off with a guilty look on our faces.

Just being able to draw this comparison has helped me get a real feeling for how much God loves us and is willing to forgive us. He just wants our love and obedience in return. Is that too much to ask? It's not too much to ask, but it is hard for us to do. While we're in church praying, Satan is out in the parking lot doing pushups. I don't think dogs have to deal with Satan. Maybe God gave them an exemption.

God gave us Jesus! He laid down *His* life for *us*. Could we do the same for Him? We may be tested someday. Be ready.

CHAPTER 11

Awakening

I've only been exposed to real Bible learning for just over three years. I'm still on fire for the Word and asking God for understanding. I'm a grateful member of a great church. However, I have recently come up for a breath of air and am seeing what I knew I might see in any organization of my fellow humans. A division in the church over doctrine as written in what we call the discipline. It all sounds very legalistic, which is something I personally don't like. I know this sort of thing has been going on since the first century as Jesus' disciples went about establishing His church.

> There are two things which are infinite, the universe and the stupidity of man; and I'm not sure about the universe.
> —Albert Einstein

Being so new to studying the Bible, I realize I only know a little and probably understand even less, and I can't quote scripture. But I think I know enough to comment on this subject with confidence.

Circumcised or Uncircumcised

In the early churches being established by Jesus' disciples, there were arguments about who would be accepted into the body of Christ as church members (Christians). This was a human failing in that it didn't follow Jesus' example. Jesus accepted everyone, even the worst sinners. The apostles themselves were no angels. Yet they presumed to make rules as to who could follow Jesus. Finally, they agreed that non-Jews didn't have to undergo circumcision to be part of the church, and they wouldn't be bound by all the Jewish laws. They should have had WWJD wristbands two thousand years ago.

It amazes me that these men spent three years listening to and learning from Jesus. They saw Him break bread with all kinds of people. Jesus healed anyone who asked for healing. The disciples were imbued with the Holy Spirit, and still, they fell into the societal thinking of the day. They wanted to put qualifiers on membership. Jesus came to demonstrate that he satisfied Old Testament prophecy and to declare that God cared less about sacrifices and rituals than right living.

A New Division in the Church

> Tolerance and apathy are the last virtues of a dying society.
> —Aristotle

Churches around the world are being challenged by the new "woke" madness infecting society today. People who call for tolerance and especially those who would twist scripture to accommodate this surging evil are exposing an extreme and dangerous weakness. People are mistakenly using the fact that Jesus sat with sinners as a way of saying He accepted evil, and they are completely wrong. However, the fact is that Jesus did spend time and even break bread with all kinds of people, but it was for healing, salvation, and instruction. He almost always said, "*Go and sin no more.*" In any case, it was always implicit that healing was a matter of casting out demons or abolishing sin. It was the "getting rid of sin" that carried the implicit instruction not to continue sinning as before.

There is also a great deal of apathy at work in all this. Satan has all his minions hard at work putting stumbling blocks in our way. Social media, the Internet, cancel culture, and every form of psychological and spiritual warfare are being used to weaken and fatigue an increasingly self-centered world. People pleasers are willing to go along to get along. This unearned tolerance and apathy are killing society today. People are unwilling to stand up for their beliefs for fear of being labeled as racist, homophobic, etc. This tells me they don't have very strong belief systems. They just sway in the wind and seem willing to allow anything. Rationalization and justification founded in false thinking have become the order of the day.

> If you don't stand for something, you'll fall for anything.
> —Alexander Hamilton
> (Hamilton is one of many people who used this quote.)

So now, many churches are being faced with the question of whether or not homosexuals should be ordained or if clergy should perform same-sex marriages. There is *nowhere* in the Old or New Testament that says homosexuality is okay. In fact, Leviticus 18:22 from the Old Testament or 1 Corinthians 6:9–10 from the New Testament, along with a few other scriptural references, state homosexuality is detestable, and anyone committing these acts will not enter the kingdom of heaven. End of discussion. I know that is an especially blunt and even harsh way to put it, but it's just the way it is. Boys are boys, and girls are girls. The fact that some people feel they have to change that for themselves is none of my business. I just don't want them insisting that I bend over backward or give up my beliefs just to make them feel better about themselves. You can't demand respect; you have to earn it. You can't legislate acceptance; it simply won't work. It never has and never will. Mankind has been trying to make laws since time began, but you just can't get people to follow all these manmade rules. When Moses received the Ten Commandments on Mt. Sinai, along with all the other Jewish laws, he came down the mountain to find all his people in a state of rebellious debauchery.

Yet our denomination and some others are splitting up over this question. It's Satan's way of dividing and conquering the church. I recently saw a reliable statistic saying that between 2012 and 2016, about thirty thousand churches closed their doors permanently. There are fewer and fewer Christians, and only 14 percent of them read the Bible daily. It seems to be getting worse since 2016.

I don't know how many demons were cast out of heaven with Lucifer, but I think they are all working overtime trying to destroy the church. How did this woke concept even get a foothold in the church? Why are we letting it divide us? It's not worthy of our time. We need to be doing the Lord's work, not letting this distract and divide us.

Could it be a misguided effort to grow the church by being more inclusive? Is it to boost revenue and look good to the secular world? If we do this, are we still true Christians? Will we allow false tolerance and apathy to defile the bride (Christian church)?

The Bible is an indivisible document. We can't claim part and twist other parts to suit a secular doctrine. We have to be willing to stand against the things we know to be wrong.

> We can easily forgive a child who is afraid of the dark; the real tragedy of life is when men are afraid of the light.
> —Plato

Some Thoughts on Homosexuality

I don't think I even need the Bible to tell me that homosexuality is wrong. It's abnormal.

Abnormal (adj)—unnatural. Also, not normal, not typical or conforming to a norm. Abnormal personality traits (Webster).

What I have to remind myself of is the old saying to "*love the sinner but hate the sin.*" I can and, in fact, do this. In my many years in AA, I've known several homosexuals. One of my friends decided to make the change from man to woman to start the new millennium in 2000. I never refused to hug her after that and never failed to support her decision in spite of the uproar it caused in our club. I don't understand it but won't turn on a close acquaintance because they made a decision for their life that others don't like. I don't have to like it, and I don't laud it, but I will accept it so long as my friend doesn't try to change me or influence others.

Let's go back to the Garden of Eden. I wrote before about how all believers believe in the Bible and therefore know God created everything and perfectly designed how it should work. One thing I mentioned was DNA. Simply God's way of creating infinite possibilities for mankind's development. However, when Adam and Eve sinned and fell from grace, they became mortal and were imperfect. Their DNA was corrupted, and thanks to a little help from Satan, many abnormalities came into being like birth defects for example. Remember, this isn't the Garden of Eden anymore. It's Satan's domain.

I believe that most homosexuals are genetically predisposed to their condition. There are others who just seem to be attracted to the same sex and are willing to pursue any depravity to satisfy their desires. There's no telling what early life experience may be at work in them. There are many well-meaning parents who have tried to deprogram or reprogram their children away from homosexual behavior. They think enough prayer or behavior modification therapy will cure them. It doesn't work. It now seems like you can't turn on the TV without seeing some form of homosexual behavior playing out in commercials or programs. TV producers seem bent on force-feeding society with the idea that all manner of abnormal behavior is okay and should be lauded.

There are no mechanisms for rule changes in the Bible. The idea that a vote can be taken and a new truth created by a majority is absurd.

> The doctrine of the atonement is to my mind one of the surest proofs of the divine inspiration of Holy Scripture. Who would or could have thought of the just Ruler dying for the unjust rebel?
> This is no teaching of human mythology, or dream of poetical imagination. This method of expiation is only known among men because it is a fact; fiction could not have devised it. God himself ordained it; it is not a matter which could have been imagined.
> —Charles Spurgeon

Atonement is extremely important, and it precedes forgiveness. The word *atonement* can be broken down as *at one with*. I don't think you can be at one with God while still breaking His law by practicing homosexuality. That's like oil and water; they just don't mix.

I'm not an advocate of any punitive action against the LGBTQIA+ community so long as they don't insist on trying to corrupt my children and grandchildren. Pedophiles should be locked up. In the Old Testament, they would probably be stoned to death. People who would try to get any child into a sex reassignment program in secret from their parents should be considered pedophiles as well. They may actually be worse.

All I can do now is pray to God that our churches wake up and get back to doing God's work and shutting out anything that doesn't fit with scripture.

> If I had never joined a Church till I had found one that was perfect, I should never have joined one at all! And the moment I did join it, if I had found one, I should have spoiled it, for it would not have been a perfect Church after I had become a member of it. Still, imperfect as it is, it is the dearest place on earth to us.
> —Charles Spurgeon

Charles Spurgeon is correct. There is no perfect church, and I'm definitely not a perfect man. I'm not saying that the LGBTQIA+ group should be prohibited from going to church. It would be shameful to say that. I have to accept that God is willing to welcome all people to His house. However, I don't see God blessing same-sex marriage. I don't believe He would approve of the ordination of these people as leaders and examples of right living. When Paul was writing to the churches, he was telling them how to organize and said that the elders and leaders should be righteous people. He said they should set a righteous example and have their houses in order. I take that to mean living according to what was declared by God as good and proper.

A LAYMAN'S LOOK AT LIFE

A Head Scratcher

For the sake of brevity, I'm going to refer to the LGBTQIA+ community as the gays going forward.

I accept that I am a sinner, and so are the gays. Are there different degrees of sin? Are the sins of gay people worse than mine? I'm inclined to say yes (of course). Why? I think that when I look lustfully at a woman it's a natural God-given response to what I see. Man is meant to be with women to have children and for pleasure. Is that different than a man looking lustfully at another man? Again, I would have to say yes because it's not natural. God has forbidden this behavior again and again, even destroying the whole world for its corruption. Noah's world was destroyed. Sodom and Gomorrah were destroyed. Babylon was destroyed. God gave Moses ten commandments, which we seem to break all the time, but we don't see God destroying the whole world on account of that.

When Jesus died on the cross, did his sacrifice cover gays too? I'm confused on this point. It seems like the answer is yes. He died for us all. My feeling, however, is that there are a few requirements to salvation. First, you must confess your sins. Then you have to ask Jesus into your life and try not to sin any more. But Jesus knows we aren't able because we're not perfect. Still, the confession and the turning over of your life to Jesus with faith in His ability to forgive and a belief that he will bring us out of this world into a new and perfect world is essential for salvation. An honest effort to do better and to stop doing the things that hurt us and God is also essential. Are practicing gays really doing anything to correct their behavior? I don't know. Only God knows. However, I think that if they are still practicing homosexuality, pedophilia, and all that other stuff, they just can't be included in salvation. Thankfully it's not up to me. When I stand before my creator, the only report card that matters will be mine. For what I did do, I am truly sorry. If I let myself think too much about my past sins, I can get pretty depressed. I'm trying to focus on becoming a better man in the here and now. I can't change or fix the past, and I no longer do the things I used to do. I still have impure thoughts and lose my temper. I still have a lot of scar tissue, which causes me to react in ways I wish that I wouldn't. Resentment and trust issues still plague me at times. All I can do is try to do better without bending my basic principles. I can't allow anyone else's ideas of what I should be like to alter who I am.

Division Is the Devil's Tool

> The cross was designed to defeat Satan, who by deception had obtained squatters' rights to the title of the earth.
> —Billy Graham

I'm developing the habit of saying, "Run to the Cross." That's the same as when I say keep it simple stupid.

I'm sorry, I just don't see any give in the simple instructions of God through Jesus Christ. Loving your neighbor as you love yourself is a tall order, and most of us just don't seem to do it very well. At least I don't. The Devil wants us divided. It's easier to conquer small groups than it is a united front of many. Our society keeps getting divided into smaller and smaller special interest groups. The most evil and insidious of these groups are Satan's special forces. They try to divide us over the smallest issues, which are often nonissues. Dragging up ancient grievances or creating new ones is a favorite tactic. There are people in the world who feel it is their right and duty to go out and take offense on behalf of people or groups of people who didn't even know they should be offended by whatever it is these clowns decide is offensive. Demanding sports teams change their names because Native Americans might be offended or stirring up resentment among one group against another by conflating past wrongs with current events are just two examples. It's getting worse every day. I think that's why many Christians feel like the Rapture is coming soon, as in this lifetime. The rate of societal decay is accelerating. The blatant display of evil is astounding and baffling. I think to a large degree Satan has been waiting for my parents' generation to pass away as well as a growing number of my generation. Schools have been indoctrinating our kids with a bunch of false information and literally trying to cancel the truth out of education. Schools are dropping real education in history, civics, geography, and other subjects in favor of woke nonsense. Meaningless tripe of no value seems to be the plan of attack. *Ignorance is not bliss! It's a snare!* Divide and conquer, confuse and deceive; that's the Devil's plan. Prophecy seems to be coming true again as it always has. I can't fight it; I just have to watch it unfold and try to sound a warning to anyone who will listen.

CHAPTER 12

Witnessing

I have spent untold hours wondering what it is I'm supposed to do in life that matters. When I started public speaking after my first wife died, I had trouble finding a subject I was truly passionate about. I was always good at speaking in front of people. I was a natural-born salesman. However, I had to believe in the products or services I sold, and that belief is what made me successful in the eyes of others. Sadly, I would often find that the product might not be as good as advertised or more often the services weren't as good as I was told they would be. As a result, I would find myself at odds with my employer and would wind up working somewhere else. I became cynical about what prospective employers were telling me when they were trying to sell me the job.

Being a salesman is the toughest, most stressful, and sometimes the most rewarding job I can think of. In my field, if you got a yes 20 to 25 percent of the time, you're usually among the very best. At least that was my experience. The problem is that there was no long-term satisfaction in it for me. I was good at it but didn't really like it. I was like the Woody Allen joke where this guy tells his friend that his brother thinks he's a chicken. So the friend says, "Why don't you get him some help?" Then the guy says, "I would, but we need the eggs."

I chose to be a salesman because it's the most money you can make without an education. I needed the eggs.

> Yes, let God be the Judge. Your job today is to be a witness.
> —Warren Wiersbe

Now, at this late stage in life, I find myself wanting to witness a lot, and it seems I'm quite passionate about it. I also find myself feeling the urgency of sharing what little I've learned. It would be very easy for me to doubt myself because of my lack of Bible knowledge; I could easily feel unqualified and keep my mouth shut, but that's not what's happening. I'm willing to speak by paraphrasing the Bible and referencing other sources just to share my experience with others. I may only know a little, but I trust what I do know, and that seems to be enough for now.

I never saw myself as becoming a proselytizer. I know how I used to react to people trying to convert my thinking and beliefs in the past. I tended to shy away from them. The more passionate they were, the further I would run. I have a lot of trust issues.

In AA we are taught that the "program" of Alcoholics Anonymous is about attraction, not solicitation. In other words, if we have a willing listener, we don't tell them what they should do or how they should think (at least not until they ask for help and are willing to follow our suggestions). Rather, we share our experience, strength, and hope with them. We talk about the spiritual and physical hole we were in and how we got out. We are more apt to share our sins and confess our wrongdoings, explaining the consequences and how they affected us before talking about the solution. This is how I think I'm going about witnessing. However, so far, I find myself sharing with people who have been saved much longer than I have and know the Bible better than I do. Living here in the buckle of the Bible belt, I feel like I'm preaching to the choir.

Trying to Speak My Truth

> To be yourself in a world that is constantly trying to make you something else is the greatest accomplishment.
> —Ralph Waldo Emerson

It may be hard to believe that a person as talkative and outgoing as I seem to be still suffers from a good deal of low self-esteem with a tendency to isolate. I'm not a very social creature. I joke about being raised by wolves, but that's because of my upbringing and all the baggage I can't seem to completely get rid of.

As a kid, I was told to "act right." Why do I have to act? What's wrong with me being me? I think Emerson is correct. It would be a great accomplishment if I could be me without needing correction or being something else. Unfortunately, I don't have very good filters or impulse control. So I have to "act" right, but I'm not a very good actor in that way. Before I retired, when I was getting ready to go to work, I would often look in the mirror and say to myself, "Show time." I had to put on my game face and go do my job whether I wanted to or not. I needed the eggs.

It's also kind of funny that we're taught to lie from an early age for the sake of being polite. The Bible said not to bear false witness, but it didn't say you couldn't tell your wife her new jeans didn't make her butt look big. These are called little white lies. However, I think that society has become so conditioned to this that the lies we tell ourselves and others are getting darker and darker. Satan's plan is subtle and insidious. We keep giving an inch here and an inch there with much faulty rationalization. This whole new "woke" philosophy is a cancer that I believe will be fatal to the world. I truly believe we are rushing head-on into the end times. People like myself (and there seem to many) believe we're in the last days before Christ comes for His bride. I think we should be feeling a strong sense of urgency about active witnessing.

As I've gotten into the Bible and my new understanding of the unearned forgiveness of Christ Jesus along with a desire to share, I find myself doing hand-to-hand combat with Satan more and more. The more I study and search out the truth the more he attacks my mind. I think the baggage I carry is Satan's warehouse. He draws from it constantly to use against me. It affects my thinking and behavior. I feel like Flip Wilson saying, "The Devil made me do it." That's not totally wrong. I have to exercise a lot of discipline to keep my mind clear of all the junk Satan throws at me. It's war, and I don't plan on losing. I'm relying on Jesus to get me through because I know I can't do it alone. I'm too weak to do it alone. It seems the stronger my faith gets the more Satan attacks.

> He who talks upon plain gospel themes in a farmer's kitchen, and is able to interest the carter's boy and the dairymaid, has more of the minister in him than the prim little man who keeps prating about being cultured, and means by that—being taught to use words which nobody can understand.
> —Charles Spurgeon

In this case, Spurgeon makes me feel like my witnessing, however simple, may be of some value. I think I write these little essays looking for some sort of approval or validation. I think critical feedback will test my willingness to either learn or stand my ground. I know it shouldn't matter, but that's just the way I am. The question is, can I leave some positive footprints on this planet before I go? Can I do something of real value before I die?

I can say for a fact that I have saved the lives of at least two people. The first was my high school roommate at a small military academy in San Antonio, Texas. I was the only guy in our barracks who would take him as a roommate. He was a bed-wetter and had a lot of emotional problems. Once, while we were getting ready for our annual government inspection, which was required for us to maintain our ROTC certification, my roomie was just standing around looking confused, and I hollered at him to get busy helping me clean the room. I tossed a wastebasket to him, and he wet his pants. I asked him what was wrong, and he said his stomach hurt. I asked him when was the last time he went to the bathroom, and he said six days. I dropped everything and grabbed him by the arm, took him to the school nurse, and explained what was going on. He was taken to the doctor and later that night had emergency surgery to remove/repair a fistula in his bowels. He could have died if I hadn't realized something was very wrong there. He did not return to school that semester, and I had the room to myself until I graduated later that year. I also got a promotion for my quick thinking.

On another occasion, I was in a chiropractor's office when a girl he had just treated called to tell him she was losing the feeling in the leg he had just worked on. I had seen her leave as I was coming in. I could overhear the conversation and butted in, asking the doctor what was going on. When he told me, I immediately told him to have her go straight to the emergency room because she might have a blood clot. The doctor followed my advice and had her go to the ER. I was right. She had a blood clot and could have lost her leg or her life had it not been caught in time. I think both of these situations were what I call "God things." I'm not sure what made me think of the solutions and gave me the ability to act with such authority to deal with the situations. It could only have been God. I'm just not that cool.

I've had some people in the past suggest things I should or could do that would be valuable or worthwhile, but I wonder if they would do those things themselves. I didn't see it, so I tended to shy away. Although there were times I would be swayed in a bad direction, and the results were always empty. I have to feel like doing something before I do it. I'm not talking about doing the things one must do for everyday living. I'm talking about things like witnessing, which is where I seem to be heading.

On that note, I have to say I'm not going to be strapping on a sandwich board and standing on street corners telling sinners to repent. I don't think I'll be looking to save the panhandlers on every street corner either. So what do I do, and how do I go about it? That's my quandary.

His voice leads us not into timid discipleship but into bold witness.
—Charles Stanley

My wife has a daughter who doesn't believe in God, at least it appears that way. We tried to bring up the subject one time, and she literally held out her hand, pursed her lips, and shook her head no. She didn't even want to hear anything about it. On another occasion, while on a family trip to Florida, I found an opportunity to voice my belief in the Bible as it related to me finding out how accurately prophecy has been fulfilled over the centuries. She seemed to listen politely, but I don't think any of what I said stuck. I wasn't pushy, and I wasn't trying to sell it. I just related how I, as a skeptic, was amazed to discover this fact. All we can do now is pray for her and her family.

Charles Stanley's admonition to bold witness sounds good but is not easy to put into practice in today's world.

If there was only a way to get more people to read the Bible and take a little time to understand the overarching story, I think the world would be a better place. The Bible is the best-selling book in the world by a huge margin, but I wonder if many people bother to read it. I bet if you gave someone a Bible with a hundred-dollar bill stuck between the pages somewhere, they would never find it unless they accidentally dropped it on the floor, and it fell out.

I hope I wasn't asleep when witnessing was the topic of any sermons in my church. So here's another quote I agree with.

> If we understand what lies ahead for those who do not know Christ, there will be a sense of urgency in our witness.
> —David Jeremiah

A Wake-Up Call

Here's where I think the church needs to step up. I think we need a strong revival among all believers, nonbelievers, and undecideds. We need to be talking about the end times as found in the book of Revelation and foretold in the book of Daniel and elsewhere in the Bible. There is nothing to fear in these books! It's a guarantee of Christ's return for His bride (the church). People get too preoccupied with all the terrible things that will happen during the seven-year tribulation period. That's *not* for us believers in Jesus Christ. We will be caught up by Jesus before all that bad stuff starts. In fact, the Rapture has to happen to start the tribulation period. There is so much support for this statement in the Bible that there should be no fear in talking about it in depth.

The church shouldn't worry about being *woke*; rather, it needs to focus on being *awake*! I don't think we can be baptized, admit our sinfulness, accept Jesus as our Lord and Savior, and then sit back and relax. I've got my ticket to heaven, so I'm good to go. Am I missing something? I see many good, loving Christian people doing many good works in the community. More than I can or am willing to do. It humbles me. However, as I struggle to find my place and calling, I can't help but think that of all the good works I see we may all be missing one very important piece, and that is witnessing. I'm not talking about a demonstration of faith with good works. That's basic and very good but too passive. I'm not talking about just witnessing about how we were saved but explaining what that means. Salvation from what? It's in the book of Revelation and supported by many other scriptures and prophesies in the Bible. We gentile Christians have a little different place in the Bible than the Jews. But we're all saved by the grace of God. This is the message we need to carry to others. Just getting people to come to believe in God is a big step. Getting them to learn how to read and trust the Bible is to me the ultimate goal.

To call yourself a child of God is one thing. To be called a child of God by those who watch your life is another thing altogether.
—Max Lucado

I agree with the first part of this quote because it's what I've been taught. Since God made everything including me, I can accept it. God doesn't make mistakes; people do, and my mistakes are too many to be counted. While I understand what he's driving at in the second half of the quote, I feel like it's subjecting me to the judgment of others and that it requires me to act in a certain way. But whose judgment should I seek to satisfy? Everybody seems to have their own measuring stick. There goes my quirky nature. On one hand, I seek approval and validation, and on the other, I don't really care what anyone thinks of me. It also speaks to my trust issues. Whom do I trust? I've wasted a large part of my life trying to please others. You know, "acting right." My trust issues come into high focus because of all the false trails I've gone down trying to "act right." I think to one degree or another, most people want to get along without conflict. However, how much are you willing to bend to achieve that peace? I believe that Satan, through his many minions, has been pushing society to bend more and more in the wrong direction. I for one have always tended to put on the brakes but have too often let off the brakes just to get along. I harbor a lot of resentment about all the compromises I feel I've been forced to make in my life. It has just occurred to me that my tendency to isolate just might be so I don't have to be somewhere I have to "act right." Other times I like where I am and don't feel like I have to act like anything other than myself.

I wrote the following on a bar napkin (which I still have) when I was about twenty years old. I guess I was wishing I had someone to understand me.

> Hello?
>
> Sometimes when I'm alone, I'm someone else.
> No one you'd know but someone you might like;
>   at least I do usually.
> But then the phone rings, and I'm someone else.
> Someone the person I'm speaking to will
>   recognize.

Maybe I really don't belong to this world, maybe I'm just stuck in it. I think I remember hearing something about being in this world but not of this world. I know I've heard it said, "*We aren't human beings seeking a spiritual experience rather, we are spiritual beings having a human experience.*" In the past that has made me wonder what reality is. Is what's going on in my head as real as what goes on in my physical world? We are told if we sin in our minds we have sinned in fact. Ouch! That thought kind of freaks me out. My brain wants to say, *I only thought about it, I didn't actually do it or would never do it*. My sinfulness is ever-present. That's the struggle and will be to the very end of my life. I know I can't fix it, and I believe Jesus has already covered all my sins even the ones I haven't committed yet.

That's still a little hard for me to comprehend. But how can a human mind comprehend the divine mind of God? I guess that's what faith is for.

I once saw Marlon Brando in an interview, and he said his last words on his deathbed would probably be, "What was that all about?" I get that.

CHAPTER 13

What Is Philosophy?

> We have philosophy professors, but no philosophers.
> —Henry David Thoreau

This quote made me laugh, but it also got me thinking too. So I took a short trip down the rabbit hole again, and what follows is a snapshot of that trip.

Webster defines philosophy in part as follows:

1. the pursuit of wisdom
2. a search for a general understanding of values and reality by chiefly speculative rather than observational means

I think Thoreau may be right. I can't think of any great philosophers from the last 100 to 150 years. I have read parts of the ancient ones like Plato, Aristotle, Socrates, Seneca, and Diogenes. These philosophers seem to have been grounded in reality and addressed the real world even if it was often in purely speculative terms. They at least tried to understand the nature of mankind and our universe. That's the nature of philosophy. They introduced new ideas and made good observations.

I don't count the more modern philosophers like Sartre, Kant, or Nietzsche to be of much value. Maybe they were too much influenced by the Renaissance, religion, and industrial age. Nietzsche

WHAT IS PHILOSOPHY?

seems like a self-pitying malcontent. He was a loser in life as far as I can tell. Although I do agree with the statement that whatever doesn't kill you makes you stronger. It seems to me, after a brief inspection, that the so-called modern philosophers are people who have too much time on their hands and come up with some of the most absurd propositions I've ever heard. They seem to have too much education, massive vocabularies (to the point of creating new words), and some extremely weird ideas about the world and reality. I think the problem is that so many of them live in the cocoon of academia, which seems to be an echo chamber of liberal lunacy. However, to be fair, some good thoughts have come from these people.

To be honest, there have been many people who express some deep insights, which are expressed in their quotes. People like Mark Twain, Albert Einstein, Dr. Martin Luther King, Ronald Reagan, John F. Kennedy, and William F. Buckley, to name a few.

Maybe we, as a society, are too busy and distracted by the modern world and all its nonsense that we don't have or make time to think deeply about reality and what's right or wrong or even what makes sense. There's the rub. There is a whole train of philosophical thought that questions the reality of reality. I just recited the idea (several people have been given credit for this quote) that we are not human beings seeking a spiritual experience; rather, we are spiritual beings having a human experience. I don't think I really believe that, but it's an interesting thought exercise. I think God made us the way we are, and we come up with these ideas while searching for God (knowingly or unknowingly).

As a kid, I used to take long solitary walks through fields and woods or anywhere I could be alone. I never really had any friends. So I walked. I liked walking through the old train yard near my house where they stored old worn-out boxcars and some cabooses. I especially liked the cabooses. I would hang out and imagine what it was like to ride around the countryside in one. I was alone but not too lonely.

I have always loved music. I think a good bit of philosophy bleeds through the lyrics. I say this because there are some songs that resonate very deeply with me. For example, I think I could say James

Taylor's song "Walking Man" describes the basic me. Although it came out years after I was a kid, it hit the heart of me. I can also say that as a young adult, Simon and Garfunkel's song "The Boxer" also struck a chord in me. The opening and closing lines are what struck me the most. Since I'm on the musical diversion, I would say the background music of my life is in Miles Davis's album *Kind of Blue* and Donald Byrd's album *New Perspectives*. From there, my life will conclude with Sarah McLaughlin singing "In the Arms of an Angel." Can music help define our philosophy or just provoke a reaction when it speaks to our philosophy? I don't know, but it was worth thinking about.

So I've decided that most if not all modern philosophy is a cloud of confusion that constructs its own reality.

Is it possible that to be of value, philosophy must speculate about what is observable? I don't know. Maybe all philosophy is just someone's opinion, in which case we're all philosophers.

> I think I am, therefore I am…I think.
> —The Moody Blues

In the end, I think people are just trying to figure it all out. This brings me back to the idea that we're all searching for God. What's the plan and meaning of all this? We can speculate all we want, but it might be easier to just read the Bible.

I think social media including TV and movies has become Satan's playground. Our addiction to social media and the rest is just a matter of degree. Some of us only tiptoe around in it, and others are up to their necks in it. I'm more of a tiptoe type. I use the Internet to find things and do research. Even then I must be a little skeptical about what I find. I don't do political, but I do research Bible teaching and ancient biblical history.

If asked what my philosophy of life is, I would say I don't know or I don't think I have one. It could be anywhere from live and let live to kill or be killed. I'm laughing right now.

CHAPTER 14

WHAT DO I BELIEVE AND WHY DO I BELIEVE IT?

Living and learning and everything that goes with all that is a very interesting journey. Now after seventy-four years on the road less traveled, I've become more comfortable with my beliefs. They have been refined over time with much thought, more learning, and a fair amount of prayer.

I remember back when I was a genius somewhere between the ages of six and my late teens, I thought that things were either right or wrong, black or white, and that the good guys always won and that life should be fair. Learning along the way that this was not the way things really were was a big disappointment. I was learning through experience that life is *not* fair.

What does it mean *to believe*? According to Webster's Dictionary, it's as follows:

1. to consider to be true or honest ("I believe the report")
2. to hold as an opinion (suppose) or ("I believe it will rain")
3. to accept something as true, genuine, or real (ideas we believe in or believing in ghosts)
4. to have a firm wholehearted religious conviction or persuasion (to regard the existence of God as fact)

And so on. You get the point.

A LAYMAN'S LOOK AT LIFE

So what does it mean *to know*? Once again, Webster's offers the following (in part):

1. to perceive directly (to have direct cognition of)
2. to have understanding of

And so on.

So what's the difference between believing and knowing? It would appear that believing is more in the nature of an opinion and that knowing is an understanding of fact. Some, if not most, people, including myself, often accept believing as the same as knowing, but I've begun to question myself on that idea. It turns out, I think, that I believe a lot more than I know. Sometimes I say I only believe something when I actually know the thing is true. The problem is when you say you know something is true, people are liable to ask you to prove it, and sometimes, depending on the claim, that can be hard to do, and I'd rather not get into an argument or debate.

As an old skydiver, I know that when I step out the door of the airplane, I'm going to go down, not up. I've said before that if I drop a piece of bread, it's going to hit the floor. So I believe in gravity because I've seen and experienced it at work.

I know if my parachutes (main and reserve) fail to open, I will definitely be seriously injured or killed. If I get hit by a speeding Mack truck, I'm going to die. I know $2 \times 2 = 4$. These are facts. I know antibiotics will kill most bacteria. I've used them, and they work. There is so much in science and medicine I've put my faith in over my lifetime that I find myself somewhat shocked and disappointed to learn that they aren't always reliable. That's my old wanting things to be black or white, true or false, or absolute popping up again.

One of the fun aspects of life is that everybody knows some things to be true and believes other things to be true. When you bring two or more people together, you often see someone who knows something that is true trying to explain to someone else that what they believe is true is, in fact, not true. I've been in situations where someone knew something that was true that proved that what

I believed was not true. That can be hard to accept, especially when trust is required or a very strong proof is needed to convince.

Generally speaking, most people seem to be most comfortable when something is universally true or has been proven over time to be true. I believe (that word again) that most people are looking outside themselves for credible sources of information.

It used to be that teachers, newspapers, and TV news were reliable. Now something has gone terribly wrong with all that. It's become almost completely politicized and full of lies. It's divisive, whereas the truth is unifying.

Parents are supposed to be reliable, even though my parents taught me things they believed were true, only to find out later they weren't true. Sometimes they would find out a thing or idea wasn't true and would correct themselves and us kids. It's amazing how much myth and legend get passed on as true. Urban legends are a good example. What fun! I think some beliefs are just a form of wishful thinking. So who or what do you trust? I believe most, if not all, people want some solid ground to stand on. They want to have faith in something outside themselves. You could say a rock upon which to stand.

I have always believed in God because that's what I was taught as a child. I thought of Him as some kind of Santa Claus with extra superpowers. I thought if I was a good boy and said my prayers, I would get what I wanted. Wrong! Like someone said, God answers all your prayers, but sometimes the answer is no. Thank God for that, or I'd have a bunch of stuff I don't really want or would regret having gotten.

So I was raised to believe in God and Jesus Christ and taught some religion. I read parts of the Bible but didn't understand. I saw the movies Like *The Greatest Story Ever Told* and *The Ten Commandments*. I could almost believe Charleston Heston was a holy man. But what did I know? I believed a lot and speculated a lot but wasn't completely sure of anything because I listened to too many opinions, many stated as facts. This is not a solid foundation upon which to stand.

Now I've reached a point where I have found a church and some information that has reshaped my beliefs and understanding of all the things I've studied, read, or been told about God, Jesus, and the Bible.

So what do I do with my religious ideas? Which parts do I believe, and which parts do I *know*, and how do I prove it? Well, I have speculated all my life about things like this. How can the stories I heard from the Bible or Sunday school teachers be true? Well, that was then and this is now, and the difference is amazing. I used to develop my own explanations based on the logic I possessed at the time. However, my logic sprang from an unfounded belief that God does in fact exist and that Jesus was a real person born of a virgin, etc. So how do I justify and explain my beliefs now since I'm so sure I'm on the right track? Well, that gets into apologetics, which is an area I'm currently unqualified to really engage in. It would require a sufficient knowledge of the Bible to be able to quote scripture in support of an argument. It would also require other proofs as support. I can refer you to the work and writings of Lee Strobel, a well-known journalist with a law degree who worked for a major Chicago newspaper. He was an atheist who, through extensive research, came to believe in and prove the reality of Jesus Christ and his story. From that, he became a believer and Christian. He wrote the book *A Case for Christ*, which also became a movie (available on Netflix and YouTube). It's easy to get lost in the weeds here, and most people don't seem to want to take the time to look at these questions deeply. It's beneficial and instructive when people like Lee Strobel take the time to thoroughly research and document the truth of the Bible.

I had a very profound personal experience when I was about seven or eight years old. One night while I was sleeping, I felt a very real and warm sense that someone was hugging me around the legs. It was a feeling of such love and assurance that I still can't describe it accurately. The next morning, I asked my mom if she had come into the room to hug me. She said no. I asked my dad, and he said no. It wasn't my brother, so who was it? My mom said maybe it was an angel. I don't know if it had anything to do with the fact that I had polio when I was four, but I was probably still wearing the special shoes I had after I recovered. Some of the other kids with me in the Texas Children's Hospital in Houston went home crippled. I walked out. After a very few years, I no longer needed the extra stout shoes and went on to run track in high school and became a skydiver, pilot, skier, scuba diver, motorcycle rider, and a good dancer.

    Later in life, I came to believe I was healed because of my faith in my mother. What I mean is that if Mommy said it, it must be true. She said I was going to get well but that the physical therapy I had to endure in the hospital was going to hurt, and it did. I was going to have high fevers, and I did. But I was going to get well, and I did. I was four, and I believed what my mom told me, so to me, that was a matter of faith producing a reality. My mom didn't heal me, but my willingness to believe her did. I'm sure she must have said many people were praying for me and so on, but my faith was in what she said would happen, and it did. I'm sure all the prayers were a factor in my healing too.

    Faith is an inside job. Nobody can have it for you, and you can't force-feed it to anybody. A person just has to believe with the same amount of faith as they have in something like gravity. Those who believed in Jesus were instantly healed by Him. That was a combination of faith and the power of God in Jesus. Those were the miracles of all time. They were repeated often enough that they should satisfy the scientific method required by nonbelievers. Why do people keep demanding that they be repeated again in our time? Is it because the miracles were so far beyond what we can do with modern medicine? Is that what modern science is trying to do—replicate these miracles with technology and artificial intelligence? Why can't they just accept that it really happened and look at the message delivered by the Great Healer, Jesus, as the rule and guide to life? It makes me think of an old Excedrin TV commercial from the '60s where a woman's mother is trying to help her in the kitchen, and she blows up at her and says, "Mother, please, I'd rather do it myself." Is that what mankind is trying to do—replicate God and the miracles of Jesus? Isn't that a little like Satan in the garden telling Adam and Eve that they can be like God if they disobey Him and eat the forbidden fruit? Is that what Satan is trying to do, lead mankind away from God and stroke his ego by telling him he can do what God can do through science? Just saying, maybe so. I'm not against science. It's good as far as it goes, but like anything, it can be used for good or evil.

Now I'm relying on firsthand experience to prove to myself whether or not what I believe, what I've read in the Bible, or learned from other readings and teachings is true. I think about how men like Sir Isaac Newton discovered an understanding of gravity and other facts. He got his inspiration for the laws of gravity by observing an apple falling from a tree. It did not hit him on the head by the way. He came up with a massive amount of knowledge through firsthand experience and extrapolation, which he tested with mathematics and theology. He wrote *Philosophiae Naturalis Principia Mathematica*, or *Mathematical Principals of Philosophy*. Sir Isaac was responsible for the beginning of the Enlightenment and a majority of the mathematics used until the theory of relativity was introduced. He developed calculus alone on his own while Cambridge was closed due to the Great Plague. He was also a theologian and wrote many papers on the Bible and theological philosophy. He believed in the observation of things in nature and learning the truth by experience and thought and used mathematics to prove it. He also believed in God and the Bible. Apparently, he saw no conflict between the two areas of his belief system: science and faith.

This brings me to one more point. What I've found and have come to believe is that some people have too much education or maybe the wrong education. Not counting the hard sciences, what I've found is that some PhDs reference other PhDs to justify or rationalize their point of view. It's almost like an echo chamber of circular logic that tries to prove itself with itself, without additional substantial truth behind it. Some scholars know so much stuff that they can't make it all hang together in a coherent argument, so they just use bits and pieces to focus on one idea at a time. If you were to follow all their teaching, you might find that they eventually wind up contradicting themselves depending on what point they're trying to make. They wind up making up new words to describe nonsensical ideas or sell some warped point of view. Where have all the real thinkers gone? Where are the originalists? I'm not referring to constitutional law but the men who had original ideas like Newton, Euclid, Einstein, Aristotle, Plato, Archimedes, etc.

I'm open-minded but not easily swayed. I like to say I'm blessed with ignorance. My head isn't stuffed full of theory and questionable philosophy. I'm just a babe in the woods looking for a way through. I've found it!

When my wife and I retired, we said we'd find a church and start going. I said okay, but felt like I was just humoring her to some degree because I had a problem with religion. Not God, religion. I thought it couldn't hurt and might actually do me some good. So I suited up and showed up. Man, am I glad I did!

We were invited to join a new Sunday school class, and the first thing we studied was a book called *The Non-Prophet's Guide to the End Times* by Todd Hampson. That may seem to be a weird place to begin—at the end. Bingo! That's exactly what I needed because he started out with the book of Daniel and explained how a large majority of the prophecies in the Bible have come to pass 100 percent accurately and the rest are yet to come but point clearly to what is written in the book of Revelation. Daniel wasn't the first prophet in the Bible, but his interpretation of Nebuchadnezzar's' dream came true in the times before Christ, and at least one in Daniel's lifetime and the other big ones were sealed until the end times.

I like proof, and I like facts. Even though I know some people try to conflate some prophecies with other events especially when they try to predict when Jesus will return for His church, I still believe that it will all come to pass in God's time and will be proven at that time. Jesus even told His disciples that neither the angels in heaven or He knew when the end time would come, but only God the Father knew. The disciples understood this because it was very much in keeping with the Galilean wedding tradition. The tradition was that the man (Jesus) would make a covenant with the prospective bride (the church) and would seal it with a ransom (giving His life on the cross). He would then return to His father's house to prepare a place for the bride, and only when the father was ready would He be allowed to return for His bride (at the Rapture). We're not meant to know everything in advance. So some people will continue to doubt until it really happens. I'm afraid that will be too late. I prefer to take the position that what has already come to pass as prophesied is a preponderance of evidence sufficient to convince or convict as some say. Therefore, I consider prophesy to be fact in advance of events. Even though we can't always understand prophesy until it comes to pass, I've seen enough to believe, and I think scholars have rendered some pretty accurate interpretations to make general predictions without exact dates. The book of Revelation is clear on many points regarding what will happen during what is referred to as the tribulation period, which will last seven years. It doesn't say when it will happen, but it will last seven years, which will have two distinct parts. You would need to look at two books of the Bible to draw a good picture of the period from Daniel's time to the end times. That would be Daniel and Revelation. Todd Hampson's book explains all this. In prophecy, many things have to happen in a specific order before the tribulation. We can see many things that have been completed and are waiting for the rest to happen. The thing is, we are running out of the prerequisite events prophesied, which leads me to believe we are getting very close to the end times. However, it is true that we have never known the time lapse between events, so I could be wrong.

While I may be unable to make a perfect and universally convincing argument to prove the existence of God and the truth of the Bible, I have come to the point where I can say for myself that I used to believe, but now *I know*! I know God is real. I don't understand his nature. I can barely grasp what infinity is like, but I've seen and experienced firsthand too many miracles, large and small, to ignore the existence of God. Again, it's what the lawyers would call a preponderance of evidence. The problem with my argument would be that many people would refuse to accept any claims I make about miracles. Miracles happen all the time, but modern man seems to want to write them off to good luck. Give me a break! What is luck? Some would say good fortune or even a blessing. However, they throw those terms around without any depth of meaning or feeling. It's like people say all the time, "Oh my god." They don't think about what they are saying and may not even believe in God but invoke His name anyway. I wonder what they are thinking. There's a strange contradiction when many people refer to God even though they claim they don't believe. They have heard of God and know that a god is supposed to be all-powerful, but they refuse to accept the one and only God because He seems to be too unbelievable, and they think there is no proof He exists. The Bible and fulfilled prophecy are all the proof you need to believe in God. I think that's Satan spreading fear, uncertainty, and doubt. People are willing to believe in all kinds of scientific claims that are based on speculative theories because so much other science is reliable but reject the Bible even though all of it is true and much of it has already been proven. A couple of my grandkids say, "Oh my god," all the time, and I know they are not taught a thing about God because their mom doesn't believe in God as far as I know. So far, she's not wanted to hear about God from me. How do I convince someone like that that God is real? I don't think I can. A closed mind receives no new information.

I said I believe in the Bible. I know that many written documents exist from hundreds of years before Christ. I know archaeologists are constantly finding proof of the existence of many people and places mentioned in the Bible. I've read many articles and watched several documentaries on this subject. The Romans, Jews, and many others were great at keeping records of events throughout history. Finally, fulfilled prophecy is all the proof I need to be convinced. What more could anyone want?

I think the trouble many people have with the Bible starts on page 1 and goes on through much of Genesis. People have trouble accepting or believing that the world, the universe, and everything was created in only six days. I get it. It's a mind-boggling thing to grasp. Who was there to witness it? How was this information passed down? I think that since Moses wrote the first five books of the Bible and had firsthand communication with God on Mt. Sinai, he received all this information about creation directly from God. This is the only and most likely logical explanation I can offer since I wasn't there. You have to remember Moses was up on the Mountain for forty days. That's plenty of time for God to tell him everything he needed to know about creation. It makes sense to me because I choose to believe what the Bible says because it has proven over time to be 100 percent reliable. Were Adam and Eve the first and only? I finally decided they were the first and only.

The Old Testament is a Jewish history with a lot of genealogy to describe the twelve tribes, their origins, etc. I think the descriptions after that are compelling. We get to see how the descendants of Adam and Eve formed new tribes and civilizations. The great city of Nineveh (Babylon) was where God tore down the tower that attempted to reach heaven. He scattered the people and confused their language, so they went to the corners of the earth and became new races of people and developed new civilizations over time. They aren't discussed in the Bible much because they aren't the main characters in the story. Sure, they exist and are mentioned as the many people around the world that Israel fought with to gain the land promised to them by God.

The information in Genesis is something that has to be taken on faith. Just like the big bang theory in science. There's no proof of the big bang. No one was there to witness it and worse there has been no direct divine communication to explain it (assuming that's what happened with Moses). The difference is that while science is excellent at explaining so much about our physical world, they are frequently having to modify or change their findings in light of new information. However, the Bible doesn't have to make changes. It is whole and complete as it stands. There is only one story and one truth. History keeps proving it.

There is one big event in the Bible that is becoming more acceptable to science, and that's the Great Flood of Noah's time. Geologists and others are seeing how it could have happened, likely did happen, and what the effects on the whole planet were. There is a very compelling documentary available on YouTube called *Is Genesis History?* If you watch the first ten to fifteen minutes, you'll be hooked enough to watch it to the end.

There is another YouTube documentary called *The Search for the Real Mt. Sinai*. These guys actually find the place where Moses had his direct communication with God. Two American men, one an investment banker and the other a retired FBI-trained police officer from California, made the incredible journey to the Middle East to see if the story was true and found what they only hoped would be there. It's real!

People who refuse to believe in God demand proof but expect it to jump out and bite them on the butt. You have to be willing to accept the possibility that God exists and then search for proof that He does or doesn't. Since you can't prove a negative, you have to be willing to believe that all the pieces of evidence being uncovered add up to the fact that God is real and the Bible is true. You can't be lazy and expect someone to hand you the *Reader's Digest* version of the facts. At the end of the day, I think we are all looking for a firm foundation. People who believe in science rely on faith a lot or else much of what they believe would collapse. I believe God gave us brains to use, and we should use them. Science keeps us busy exploring God's handiwork. Religion keeps us busy trying to live a good life. There is no reason they shouldn't coexist in harmony. Neither one disproves the other. In fact, I think one can lead us to the other. By that, I mean science is actually leading us to God.

So let me say this: science offers us facts about our physical world but doesn't answer the question of why we're here and what comes after we die. Religion, at least my Christian religion, tells me how I got here, why I'm here, what I'm supposed to do, and what will happen after my physical body dies. If you have awareness, intelligence, and ask questions, then you have a spirit. We all have a spiritual mass and seem to be seeking the answers to our existence. I believe God is like spiritual gravity drawing us (our spiritual mass) toward Him. Your spiritual mass depends on your faith and spiritual compass. If your compass points true north, you're headed in the right direction. If it points due south, you might be headed the wrong way. Check your heading!

So what do I believe, and why do I believe it? I believe in God, and I believe the story the Bible tells is true and complete. I believe these things because I feel there is sufficient proof to support my belief. Jesus was a real person. I believe He was conceived by the Holy Spirit (which is God also) and that he was wholly human and wholly divine.

Here I want to insert my speculation/belief on the mechanics of the virgin birth of Jesus for nonbelievers. There exists in science the fact that some reptiles, invertebrates, and even some birds can spontaneously reproduce asexually. It's called parthenogenesis. Since I believe God can and does cause everything in nature, I see no reason he couldn't cause Mary to have this ability but slightly different from reptiles. When any organism reproduces this way, you get an exact copy of the parent because there is no outside DNA involved. In Mary's case, she got God's son Jesus. The mechanics existed, but the result was a one-time, one-of-a-kind expression of God in man. The Holy Spirit produced not a copy of Mary but God in man as Jesus. The Holy Spirit replaced the other DNA required to create Jesus. If you can believe in the possibility of parallel universes or black holes, why not this too? It's called faith. If you believe in science, you already have faith in science, which you believe to be fact. In many cases, it is fact. Science is not wrong, just incomplete. As I said, science looks at God's handiwork and studies the mechanics of it but can't really explain its origin without a lot of speculation and faith.

Some Christians may not appreciate my attempt to put a scientific explanation on a divine event like the virgin birth of Jesus. But the whole process of reproduction is divinely conceived by God, whether sexually or asexually or by simply His will. Some people like to imagine God simply saying Mary would give birth to Jesus by His word alone without any fancy scientific explanation. That's fine and is just as possible. I believe God's word was in the Holy Spirit. I'm just trying to show nonbelievers how a virgin birth *is* possible in their worldview. Jesus was fully human and fully divine. Something had to happen to start the chain of events of cell division and the formation of a baby in Mary's womb without sex. One only needs to believe in God's spirit working in the human realm no matter the mechanics. It's all a mystery anyway.

CHAPTER 15

THE BIG SEARCH

I believe we are born searching. Just look at the eyes of a newborn as they scan their environment for the first time with wide-eyed innocence. Everything is new and strange. They haven't yet developed enough to put names to things or people, but they are like sponges soaking everything in. As we grow up, we begin to ask questions about *everything*. How many times have you heard kids ask why or what's that? It can make you a little crazy, especially when you either don't know the answer or the answer is too complicated for their age and understanding. Lord, help us the first time they ask where babies come from or about sex. This is a very sensitive subject, and I won't go into it too much. Since I never had kids of my own (I raised one set of stepchildren, a seven-year-old girl and an eleven-year-old boy when I got them, and it never came up for me). I only imagined later in life how I might have explained it, but it would have depended on the age of the kid asking and I'll leave it at that.

The point is we humans are always looking for answers to questions. That's what the early philosophers were doing, and many great thinkers came up with some interesting observations about nature, human nature, science, medicine, society, and religion. I'm talking about how human beings have always looked for ways to explain what they observe in the world around them and their interactions with other human beings. We all want to know how things work at least to some extent. Some just want to know where the light switch is while others think about how to create light. It started with fire and wound up with what we have today. Different disciplines of study developed over time depending on the interests of different people. Physics, math, and astronomy for some; medicine, biology, and anthropology for others; philosophy and religion for others; and many more. One thing they all had in common was a lot of superstition, myths, and gods created for each category. There was a god for weather, fertility, crops, war, and so on. People were making idols to look like whatever they thought these gods should look like. They were creating gods after their own imagination. They also gave these gods many human attributes like anger, jealousy, revenge, you name it. They were fickle gods, unreliable and unresponsive. Despite people claiming unwavering allegiance to these gods, they knew they were unreliable and fickle. I think that's why so many people refused to even consider believing in one all-powerful universal God as the cause and creator of all things. They had already had too much experience believing in man-made gods to believe that there could be one superior to anything they had ever imagined. They wanted to look for better, clearer explanations for the world they lived in. The stories in the Bible and the testimony of the people who lived and observed all these miracles in real time were just too hard to believe. So science evolved, and knowledge grew. Fortunately, there were many who did believe in one all-powerful God, and these were the Jews, God's chosen people. However, their faith only came from seeing firsthand God's power demonstrated on earth. God chose certain people to carry His message and perform many demonstrations to prove His existence. He chose messengers called prophets to tell the people how they should believe and worship Him. God even appeared to special people and communicated directly with them to carry His message. People like Noah, Elijah, and Moses, to name a few. However, even when people heard and believed they continued to disobey God's commands, it would be hard for nonbelievers to be convinced when they saw believers continue to break God's commands and live just like they were living. How could there be a God when His chosen people suffered the same as they suffered? If they had applied a little scientific method to their observations, they would know that all the believers' sufferings were a result of the fall in the Garden of Eden. They would have seen by reading the Bible how the sinful nature of mankind produced repeatable and reliable results. Repeatable in that sin always led to failure and reliable just because the results were always the same. It wasn't until after Jesus lived, performed miracles, died on the cross, and rose from the dead that people had a way out of the suffering for the sins they committed. They only had to believe that Jesus died to cover their sins, and if they would admit their wrongs, repent, and try to live as Jesus would have them live, they could be free from all the guilt and much of the difficulty of life. They could have faith in a better life to come, in eternity with Jesus in heaven. The problem is that many people have just become too skeptical to accept this truth. They have become gun-shy about any proposition that relies on an unseen spiritual power. They can believe in unseen gravity because it's physically powerful and ever-present. Spiritual power is ever-present but requires input and effort to maintain, and it can't be felt physically. It requires faith. Everybody has faith in something they just need to be willing to take a chance and let God in. The Bible and fulfilled prophecy are the truth and proof people can rely on *if they would only read the Bible* and get some solid Bible instruction.

    I think one of two things can happen in a person's life for them to have the ability to believe. One, they can be raised in a religious environment and taught about Jesus and salvation. This would include a firm foundation in Bible study with an understanding that scripture predicts and proves history. In other words, the Bible is a true story. The second way is for someone to be so beaten down by life and their own sins that they become willing to try anything, including surrendering their life and will to God. In AA, we call this hitting bottom. We say turn your life and will over to the care of God as you understand him. That means you have to accept that there is a supreme being of a spiritual sort that is all-powerful, true, and reliable. I think people who gain faith by the first method stand a better chance of losing or coming to question their faith during their lives as they collide with life's difficulties in the material realm. People who come by faith in the second case are more likely to hold it close because they have already tried everything else, and it didn't work. I believe in being forged in the fires of adversity. That was my personal experience, so I'm always somewhat in awe of people who were raised with faith. They probably have their own cross to bear, it's just not as self-destructive as my life of alcoholism and depression was. I do feel like having come so close to death so often, I might have a stronger sense of gratitude for my salvation than someone who hasn't been as thoroughly forged by life's fire as I have. I spent a lot of time searching and reaching for meaningless material things and personal gratification. My original road less traveled was a dead end. Finally, I had to rely completely on God because there was nothing else. Oh, I wish I knew then what I know now.

CHAPTER 16

Resentment and Forgiveness

You may have heard it said that resentment is the poison *I* drink to kill *you*. How true that seems to be. I think resentment has the power to kill me. Resentment can make a person physically and mentally ill. It's a corrosive thought pattern that takes up a lot of real estate in your head if you let it. For me, it used to lead to thoughts of revenge. I would come up with all sorts of scenarios where I would have the power to do all sorts of harm to the person or institution I was resentful toward. There were also principles and doctrines with which I disagreed, like some laws or cultural ideas. I would dream up ways to eradicate them by some magical power I would never possess. Resentments often gave me a way to avoid looking at what part I may have played in whatever situation I was dealing with. When I started getting honest with myself and looked at how I played a role in the situation or relationship turning sour, I began to let a lot of resentment go. In fact, that honesty made me humble and somewhat embarrassed and, in a few cases, guilt-ridden for a while. In AA, we have a process for making amends to the people we have had difficulty with. People we have wronged are often willing to forgive us and accept our apologies. For those who don't or won't, we just accept that we've done our part and ask God for forgiveness. It's funny how I always used to cry for justice in my resentments. My idea of justice was me getting even with who or whatever I was resentful toward. After I got sober and let God into my life, I began to beg for forgiveness rather than demand justice. If had gotten justice, I'm pretty sure I would not have liked it.

Some people, including myself, seem to hang on to resentments like family heirlooms. We seem to treasure them. It seems like our resentments become a part of our identity. They can define us in ways that are unattractive and cause others to shy away from us. Resentments can twist our whole outlook on life and the world around us. This is likely to put us in conflict with much of life and can cause even more resentment to pop up. We start to feel sorry for ourselves and wonder why the world and life don't treat us fairly. Resentments can be like a big tattoo in the middle of your back. You never really get to see it, but it's always there, and getting rid of it will be time-consuming and painful. I think the fear of the pain that goes with getting rid of resentment must be overridden by a strong desire to escape the pain of hanging on to the resentment. Of course, there is also the probability that one would have to admit that their basis for holding on to the resentment might not have been valid in the first place. In my case, I often found that I had a part in whatever conflict caused me to have resentment. That didn't include cases where I had been wronged by another person where I was not at fault like the sexual abuse when I was a kid. I was the victim, not the perpetrator. It took a long time to push the guilt of those experiences aside and accept that my innocence had been betrayed. I had allowed my trust and curiosity to lead me astray.

The resentments I had toward my brother and my dad were the hardest to get rid of, and I found it very hard to forgive them for a long time. My brother was a user. He tended to view people only in terms of their possible usefulness to him. He fit every definition of a narcissist. He would do some very nice and generous things, but they always seemed to have strings attached. Then dumb old me would be like Charlie Brown to his Lucy. He'd gain my trust enough for me to run up and kick the ball, and then at the last minute, he'd jerk it away so I'd fall on my butt. He thought it was funny.

My dad was an alcoholic and used to beat us as kids. He also dished out plenty of verbal abuse. His cursing could make a drunken sailor blush. He also showed excessive favoritism to my half-brother so it wouldn't look like he was giving me (his natural son) too much attention. He actually admitted it to me later in life by way of an apology. Too little and too late for me to care or accept. I always knew it anyway. Oh well, so much for my dysfunctional family drama. Resentment of family can be one of the most difficult hurdles to clear in life.

Now we have to talk about forgiveness. Yikes, this isn't easy. I'm a recovered alcoholic and suffer from clinical depression. I think I had undiagnosed childhood depression, which led to my alcoholism. Then again, it could have just been genetic. I was getting sips of beer as a toddler. When I was a little kid, I would drink from unfinished beer bottles or cocktail glasses left on the tables after a party. I like to say I was just a social drinker until I turned thirteen. That's when I got a job selling newspaper subscriptions door to door like I had done when I was younger. But now I was making some serious money for a kid. Twenty to thirty dollars a week or more in 1962 was a lot. Kids my age didn't run around with that kind of money in their pockets. This gave me the money I needed to buy beer for myself. I would go with some older friends to a part of town where we could always find some guy outside a liquor store to buy whatever we wanted in return for buying him whatever he wanted. I didn't drink every day but got drunk as often as I could. I would spend the night with friends who had much less supervision than I had, and we would find a way to get drunk. Sometimes I would stash a pint of rum at home then buy a quart bottle of Coke on the way to the bus stop. I would drink part of the Coke and then top it off with rum. I would take it on the school bus and drink it on the way to school. Other kids would help drink it too, and we never got caught. By the time I graduated high school, I was a full-blown alcoholic. This was what helped warp my thinking and view of life. Even though I was basically a good guy and always just wanted to have fun, I stormed through life on autopilot. I went whichever way my nose pointed. I never expected to live past thirty anyway, right? However, by the time I was thirty-two, I started to realize that the footsteps I kept hearing behind me were those of the stark reality of life. I had to come up with a new plan to keep making the kind of money that allowed me to live the lifestyle that I wanted.

My business partner and I were on the outs, and business was falling off rapidly in 1979–1980. I had been writing and performing stand-up comedy during that year, but in spite of getting an invitation to the Comic Strip in Los Angeles, I was too afraid I couldn't make it out there. I think I felt like if I went out there, I would be lost forever (whatever that meant). So I got a safe job with benefits and stayed in Houston. In December of 1983, I got sober and joined AA. That's when I had to start looking at my resentments and trying to figure out how to forgive the people and institutions in my life that had caused me so much pain.

Forgiveness is so hard because you can say you forgive but you can't seem to forget. When I'm reminded of some past hurt, I tend to refeel the pain, and the resentment starts to come back. It can be a vicious cycle. If I'm lucky, I can put aside the resentment long enough to try and reason my way through to forgiveness. I do this by trying to recognize that I'm not perfect and have done things that have undoubtedly caused resentment in others toward me. I try to realize that whoever it is I'm resentful toward probably suffers from some of the same thoughts, motives, and feelings I have had in the past. I may even see where I committed the same offense against someone else that was done to me. However, my worst resentments are about things I never did to anyone else, which makes it harder for me to relate and therefore forgive.

I read a helpful quote recently. It said, *"Forgive others not because they deserve forgiveness, but because you deserve peace."* Easier said than done, but true nonetheless. I think in some cases, I just have to accept that the scar tissue won't ever go away, and I have to remind myself that I survived whatever it was I resent, and it's in the past. Maybe if I remain willing to forgive, someday, I may actually be able to let go. This requires a lot of prayer on my part. I ask God to help me let go of anger, resentment, fear, and guilt. I like the saying, *"Let go and let God."* It works if you can let go! I rarely let go of anything that didn't have claw marks all over it.

CHAPTER 17

DEPRESSION AND SIN

There are, in my layman's view, two kinds of depression. There is situational depression and clinical depression. Everybody suffers from situational depression from time to time. If you lose a loved one or pet, for example, you can be sad and depressed. However, clinical depression is only experienced by some people who have an imbalance in their brain chemistry. I have clinical depression, and it is hell on earth. I wouldn't wish it on my worst enemy. It's worse than my alcoholism because all I had to do with alcohol was stop drinking it and follow a few simple guidelines laid out for me in AA.

There is no blood test for clinical depression that can tell you exactly what chemical your brain needs. Science has come up with some pretty good medicines for it, but you still have to start out as a guinea pig to find out which one works for you. Then if you find the right one or ones, they may stop working in a few years, and you have to go back through the guinea pig phase again. Then there are side effects to deal with. Suffice it to say, clinical depression is no fun.

So what's all this got to do with sin? First, we have to accept that sin is a real thing, not just some church term to make you feel guilty for doing bad things you probably already know you shouldn't do. I think somewhere in the back of my mind, I wanted to shy away from the word *sin* because it seemed to carry with it an aura of thunder and lightning and fire and brimstone. None of this is necessarily wrong, but it has a such negative effect that most of us would rather not admit our sinfulness. Why? If we talk about or admit sin, we are putting ourselves in the realm of religious belief.

Webster's defines *sin* in part as,

1. an action that is or is felt to be reprehensible
2. an often-serious shortcoming
3. a transgression of the law of God

Many people today are not religious or even close to it. I think most people know who God is or is supposed to be but don't want to accept that He is real or that religion has value.

This is where I go back to the Bible and the idea of prayer and meditation. There are so many different interpretations of the Bible and so many doctrines out there that we find ourselves not knowing who or what to believe. I get it. I was somewhat the same way. Much of what I learned when I was younger was not biblical but dogma. That's what I liked about AA. We are told we have to be willing to turn our lives and our wills over to the care of God *as we understand Him*. What a lot of religion has done is remove the power of choice in how we can relate to and have a relationship with God. Dogma has clouded the path we need to follow. I like the following quote because I think it describes how dogma works.

> A false conclusion, once arrived at and widely accepted is not easily dislodged; and the less it is understood, the more tenaciously it is held.
> —Connor Cantor,
> German mathematician 1845–1918

So you don't have to beat yourself up or engage in self-flagellation because of dogma to accept God is real and that you can develop whatever relationship you need with Him. Everybody sins. Nobody is exempt. It's just in our nature.

Therefore, I think sin can cause much situational depression. I also think sin can, to some extent, cause or at least exacerbate clinical depression. I have read that it's possible that repeated sin and a sin-filled life can shift a person's brain chemistry to some degree. Any repeated action can become a habit, and some habits are harmful mentally, physically, and spiritually. Remember sin is baked into our nature already. Spirituality, developed by studying the Bible and accepting that there is a God and that he loves us, is the way out of a sin-filled life. It's no guarantee that we won't sin again because we will. It's just the best way I know to avoid sin and the guilt and the shame that goes along with it. Once we can get rid of as much shame and guilt as possible the happier we will be. We will be depressed less often and recover quicker when we are depressed.

> The Bible is the only book whose author is always present when one reads it.
> —anonymous

Having something reliable to believe in that attaches to your innermost being is more important than all the facts of the scientific world. Science is great, but it's not soul-satisfying. It won't fill the hole in your soul, just the hole in your education. But remember it tends to change with new information. The Bible doesn't change. Find a church that supports your understanding of God and who he is to you.

You're not going to find a perfect church that exactly matches your understanding of God. What you need to look for is one where you can feel the sincere welcoming love of the people who go there. So go to church. Make new friends. Develop your own understanding, but be willing to learn what there is to learn from people who have studied the Bible. Find Christian literature that teaches solid Bible history and explains the Bible. I've already made some good suggestions in that area. Pray for guidance and understanding.

Remember the Truth shines in its own light.

> There is something of a civil war going on within all of our lives. There is a recalcitrant South of our soul revolting

against the North of our soul. And there is this continual struggle within the very structure of every individual life.
—Rev. Martin Luther King Jr.

I like this quote because it addresses for me the source of much depression. We make thousands of decisions every day. They crowd our minds and can cause confusion and conflict. When you add the outside pressures of the world and all the bad news we have to hear about, it's no wonder so many people duck into a corner where they can play on Instagram or other nonessential pastimes just to get some relief when depression sets in. Try finding a quiet place, preferably outdoors, where you can pray and meditate. Leave the material world behind (even your cell phone). I like being outdoors so I can see and be in the middle of God's creation. I'm talking about a park, not a parking lot. Although I have gone out to my car and sat in the parking lot at work so I could pray and get away from the phone and my desk for a while. I don't smoke, but I treated it like a smoke break. Just let go of the stress, and count your blessings. I believe stress is the most prevalent and damaging health condition in the world today. I believe it leads to all kinds of diseases like depression, eating disorders, obesity, heart problems, and cancer, to name a few. I like to say, *"It's mind over matter. If you don't mind, it don't matter."* I think many people stress over the possible consequences of their problems more than the problem itself. Ask yourself if it's a problem you can fix. If so, face it and fix it. If you can't fix it, give it to God, and wait to see what happens. If you can accept that there is a God who is all-powerful and infinite and that you can rely on Him and trust His will for you, you can get rid of so much stress and depression, you won't believe it. What have you got to lose, just your mind or your life. Do some research, ask for help and guidance in a mainstream Christian church, and make a leap of faith. Consult a properly qualified medical professional to see if you have clinical or situational depression. Sometimes depression is the source of the problems we face, not the result of the problems. What I mean is, I have often awakened in the morning feeling depressed. I'm sleepy-headed, grumpy, slow-witted, and generally not wanting to face the day ahead. I may have been in a job I hated or worked with some people I didn't like. I may have felt like I should be making more money. Being a salesman most of my life, I may have had a burdensome quota to fulfill or a potential sale pending I felt I couldn't afford to lose. In that condition, it was possible I might make some bad decisions based on selfish wants that caused problems that should never have happened. This could cause deeper depression. It's a painful spiral. Regardless of the cause, I needed relief. Back in the day, it was booze, recreational drugs, and when I was single, going to nightclubs looking for women. That's not a soul-satisfying way of life.

We all have a spiritual civil war to fight in our lives, so seek your better angels, and fight the good fight. I mean, gee whiz, it's only a battle for your soul, right? Isn't that worth a little effort? In the end, it's all about what happens after we die. So much of what goes on in this life is of little consequence really. We all strive to have a good life however we define it. Some of us want a big house, fine car, money, and prestige. Some of us just want a roof over our head, enough to eat, and some peace of mind. I think we all want security and freedom. However, at the end of the day, we can't take any of it with us. So I think it becomes necessary to put things in perspective. I know as I've gotten older, I've greatly reduced my aspirations for the material things in life. I've come to realize that the more things you own, the more things own you. You have to spend a lot of time and money to maintain the things you clutter your life with. You probably worry about all these things. How do I maintain them, when do I find time to fix, clean, or otherwise care for them? How can I afford to replace something I spent too much money on in the first place, or how can I get the things I don't have? Even if you have a lot of money and don't have to worry too much about such things, I bet you may find that none of it really fills that hole in your soul. I've known a lot of people who have a lot of money, and they weren't really happy because they could always have whatever they wanted. They never had much to look forward to. I remember another movie line where the main actor tells a younger man going through a personal struggle that "*Happiness is just having something to look forward to.*" It makes me think of that old Peggy Lee song "Is That All There Is." So what's it all about? There has to be more than this life, and I believe there is. That's a lot of what the Bible is about. It talks about a life everlasting and an eventual return to a new garden of Eden. No more pain, fear, or suffering. Try to let go of the things you can't control. That's one of the best stress relievers I know. It can eliminate a lot of depression and help keep us away from the sinful actions that we commit to get out of whatever problems we have. Think about this.

> God grant me the serenity to accept the things I cannot change, the courage to change the things I can and the wisdom the know the difference.
> —"Serenity Prayer" from Alcoholics Anonymous

That's a good prayer and good advice. I'm reminded of an old story you've probably heard about the little boy who has two puppies that are always fighting. One pup is good, and the other is bad. The kid asks his grandpa which dog will grow up to be the stronger. His grandpa says, "Whichever one you feed the most."

Don't feed the bad thoughts you have; they will only grow stronger. Don't wallow in morbid reflection and resentment toward other people or institutions in your life. Look for ways to put yourself in peaceful surroundings. Listen to the birds sing, walk outside, or sit somewhere outside that's peaceful. Listen to calming music. Learn to pray.

That's the cool thing about faith. If you can believe in God and the overarching story of the Bible and trust that everything bad going on in your life is only temporary, you can find a way out of depression. If you need medication to help, take it. Just remember medicine only helps with brain chemistry. It doesn't help with situations that cause all the other problems in life. That's a God thing. Dump all of that stuff on God; He can handle anything. Don't be afraid to change your circumstances to get away from the things that are hurting you. Leave bad friends and bad habits behind, and quit living in the past. Try to focus on today, and make it the best you can. This is great advice; I wish I could follow it all the time, but I can't. It's a process, not an event. I'm getting better at it, and I believe it's all because I've finally found a new spiritual reality that I can trust. That all stems from the Bible and learning what it means to and for me. This is not a result of some religious brainwashing or wishful thinking. It's real! It's a result of taking time to read the Bible and read about the Bible. Going to church is about fellowship and worshiping God. The real journey to faith is extremely private and personal and is an inside job between just me and God. I like the fellowship because it allows me to learn more from other Christians who have studied the Bible longer than I have. But that doesn't necessarily mean they outrank me in the spiritual realm. It just means they've been using their spiritual tool kit longer than I have and may know more ways to use it. I need to learn more and add to mine. More tools and more ways to use them. Good stuff! I've also made a lot of new friends and really love them.

Ask God for the power of discernment. When you are in the right place among the right people, I believe you will feel it and know it. It's a wonderful thing and a great feeling. Remember earlier when I was talking about always looking for an honest man? I said when I finally found one in the mirror, I began to find myself among other honest men (and women). This has helped me develop a new level of trust along with the ability to deal with situations where that trust is violated. Those violations rarely happen because I'm dealing with more trustworthy people. When my trust is violated, I don't have to dwell on it or let it mess with my head because I know everybody sins, and I have the ability to let it go. I shouldn't be surprised when it happens because I'm dealing with imperfect humans. It will only hurt for as long as I hold on to it. Remember, "Let go and let God?" and "If you don't mind, it don't matter"? Nothing can break you when you have faith and practice it.

CHAPTER 18

THE BIG PROMISE

So what's the big promise for us Christians? It's life eternal with Jesus in heaven, right? Revelation in the Bible says that at the Rapture, we will be caught up in heaven with Jesus but will return to earth with Him when He comes after the tribulation to defeat Satan and all sinners once and for all. Before the final defeat of Satan, there will be the millennial kingdom where all those who survived the tribulation and were converted to Christianity will live in harmony and repopulate the earth. Those of us who were caught up in the Rapture will have various assignments during this period, and then eternity will occur. So here is where I used to get confused. Please forgive this diversion, but I have to confess I have had these thoughts from time to time in the past before I came to my new understanding of the Bible and the meaning of my salvation. Remember John was shown by an angel from heaven all that would come to pass. One has to realize what he wrote was his observation of the divine and miraculous as viewed by a first-century human mind. He described many things as "being like" something he could describe. I'm still learning to understand what he was saying. Like so many humans, I want details I can understand with my semi-scientific mind. So years before I discovered the Bible, I used to have a few silly questions about the hereafter. Will I be in heaven or on some new and improved earth? I had some other silly questions like will the earth get overpopulated because the saved will live forever? Will there be barbecue, steaks, bacon, and ice cream?

I wonder if non-Christians and nonbelievers (atheists) think believing in God is a waste of time. They may think eternity in heaven will be boring without any fun or pleasure as we currently know and understand such things. They may feel like giving up all their earthly pleasures for some nebulous spiritual future in the hereafter, this big promise, is just not worth it. Many people think the here and now is all there is and want to get the most they can out of it.

This is where faith comes in. I can't have faith in fairytales. I want some hard evidence to convince me that what I'm putting my trust in is worth whatever sacrifice I might have to make in order to receive the promised reward. That's why I keep going back to the Bible. It tells me there is no amount of work or good deeds that will get me into heaven. It's by grace we are saved, and that is a gift from God if we believe in Jesus. I've had some people tell me that the Protestant Bible is incomplete because it doesn't contain all the books it could have like the Apocrypha. The New Testament in the King James, NIV, and other interpretations contain many references to the Old Testament, which had long been accepted as true and accurate accounts of Jewish history. Especially important in the Old Testament were the prophets because many of their prophecies came true before and after Christ. These prophecies included the foretelling of John the Baptist and Jesus Christ. They told of the virgin birth of Jesus and many other things that came to pass 100 percent accurately. So the Bible only contains those books that God wanted included based on their provability, relevancy, and accuracy. The Bible is God's way of communicating with mankind what He is like and what He expects from us. It shows how he manifested Himself in Jesus so that we could see how He wants us to live. It also allowed Him to prove that He has real power to heal and even overcome death. For a book to be included in the New Testament, it had to be written by someone who was an apostle, closely associated with an apostle, or had observed firsthand Jesus' works and miracles. While the Old Testament predicts the New Testament, the New Testament proves the Old Testament. It is also true that there are many outside historical sources that support and prove the truth of the Bible. This is why I trust the Bible and accept that no matter how many doubts or silly questions I may have had about what's coming to all believers in Christ, I trust that it's going to be better than anything I can conceive. I don't think I'll be bored; I just have no idea what I'll be doing with an eternity at my disposal. I'm sure God will tell me. I certainly don't want the other scenario where I burn in hell forever.

So what do I have to give up in order to be a member of the Christian community? The answer is not all that much. In AA, we are told we must be willing to go to any lengths to recover from our alcoholism. That seemingly hopeless state of mind and body, which had kept us in misery for so long is what we were trying to get rid of. I found during my forty years of sobriety that the lengths I had to go to were not that great. I gave up drinking and drugs. I gave up lying to myself and others. I gave up trying to be something I wasn't to make myself look and feel better. It never worked anyway. I made a complete confession of all the sins I could remember and made a vow not to repeat them, and I turned my life and my will over to the care of God *as I understood Him.*

This was a new God. This God was a loving and forgiving father, unlike any earthly father I could have wished for. This wasn't the scary God in white robes scowling down on me from some cloud and throwing lightning bolts. I could talk to this God and believe He heard me. He didn't talk back, and we didn't have a hotline open, but He did change my heart and outlook on life. This God showed me intuitively how to handle situations that used to baffle me. This is what AA gave me. When I finally started reading the Bible honestly and looking at it as a true history book plus reliable prophecy, I began to have a whole new outlook on life.

So what more did I have to give up to become a part of the Christian community? The answer is nothing. Instead, I got to be in a group of people who studied and believed in the Bible and were willing to share that knowledge with me. I got an understanding of Jesus' sacrifice on the cross for me. I learned about the Bible and many things about life in the first century. I found other sources of information, which helped me understand how to prove the reliability of the Bible. So in the end, I gave up nothing I hadn't already given up; rather, I got an unexpected and undeserved reward by receiving the Word of God through the Bible. I received a guaranteed salvation I don't deserve and could never earn. I have new and different friends now. I still have some of my old friends. It's just that I've added a whole new group of people whom I love and appreciate. So that's the Big Promise in a nutshell. Remember, I like to say, "Keep it simple, stupid." I run to the Bible because I can rely on it. When I catch myself having problems or doubts in life, I just turn to the Bible for comfort and reassurance. Sometimes it's just Satan trying to create problems in my life. I now have a way to fight him and a way to test the value of the things I hear. Like I've said many times before, the truth shines in its own light. Two times two is still four, and everything is alright already.

CHAPTER 19

Wrapping Up

Many religions teach that there is a life after death. Some say you climb some sort of ladder to better and better circumstances if you live properly at the original level. In other words, you earn your way up. However, if you mess up a level, you go backward, or you can be reincarnated as something else in the next life. I'm still learning more about being a Christian. Besides, I wouldn't want to be reincarnated because with my luck I'd come back as me. Uh, no thanks. Been there, done that, and don't need another T-shirt.

We Christians are told via the Bible that if we confess our sins and profess our faith in Jesus, we will have an eternal life in heaven with God and Jesus. This is because God chose to come to earth as a human in the form of Jesus Christ, His only son. This was in order to demonstrate His power by healing many hundreds of people of every kind of illness and other things like blindness, deafness, and even death. Jesus was a Jew, and the miracles He performed were made for the Jewish people so that they would begin worshiping God in a new and different way from the blood sacrifices required by the laws of Moses. Jesus came to let them know God didn't care for all the sacrifices and burnt offerings as much as he wanted people to worship Him and to love each other. The sacrifices he wanted were the personal sacrifices of individuals to serve and help their fellow man, especially widows and orphans.

The Jews are a stiff-necked people by their own admission. Back then, they were always complaining and judging God. Remember *Sa-tan* means "judge." He was constantly stirring up discontent and division among the people. (He's still doing it today.)

When John the Baptist first saw Jesus coming down to the river Jordan, he declared, "Here is the Lamb of God."

A voice from heaven (God) said, "This is my son in whom I am well pleased."

For three years, Jesus traveled throughout Israel preaching and performing miracles. He was teaching a new way to treat our fellow man with compassion, generosity, and love. He ate with sinners and all kinds of people the Pharisees considered beneath them. Jesus read from the Torah and never blasphemed or did anything to give offense to the Jewish leaders. What He did do was perform miracles including raising the dead. Many of these miracles were witnessed by the Jewish elite. I think they would have welcomed Him to be among their number if he hadn't constantly pointed out their sins and hypocrisy. He also drew many followers by showing them they didn't have to live by all the laws of the church elite. Jesus made Himself a servant and was humble in all ways. So the Pharisees conspired to kill Him. He was bad for their corrupt business practices.

As foretold in prophecy, Jesus went to Jerusalem to celebrate Passover. This is where he was betrayed and condemned to crucifixion. He was the Lamb of God. His blood sacrifice on the cross was to spare all who believed in Him. His blood was like the blood on the doorjambs in Egypt before the exodus. It promised life eternal in heaven with Jesus and God.

Before his death, Jesus instructed His disciples to go out and spread the good news. But first, they had to witness Jesus raised from the dead as proof of His Godhood and to prove that through Him and Him alone, anyone can obtain eternal life. After seeing Christ Jesus alive in the flesh, the disciples and many other firsthand witnesses could give testimony about this amazing miracle.

At the Pentecost, the disciples received the power to perform miracles like Jesus. They were also sent out to establish churches among Jews and Gentiles alike. Paul was a major figure in bringing Jesus' story to the Gentiles.

So long story short, I think if anyone is willing to read the Bible with an open mind, and if they can see the Truth shine through, they are in the right place to put their faith in Jesus. If you can become willing to believe that there is more to life than just this material realm we live in, then you are ready to take the next step by faith in Jesus. We are all sinners, and there is no way we can do enough good works, pray enough, or pay enough to earn our way into heaven. The grace of God is a free gift through which you receive salvation and a seat at the table in heaven.

The first death we will all experience. The second death is the one where nonbelievers who would not accept Christ Jesus will experience permanent death, which is an exclusion from heaven and God's presence. It is written that these people will be in hell with Satan and all his followers.

I've read a lot of things and heard a lot of opinions about what heaven and hell are supposed to be like. But let's face it: nobody knows, and all the human interpretations of the Bible or any other source material will never be able to explain it completely. All I know is that I believe in God and all his works, and therefore I believe in Jesus and His promise. I don't need to know everything in advance because, like so many things in my life, I find that when I just let go and leave the results up to God things work out better than I could ever have imagined. My own life and the fact that I'm still alive after all I've done right and wrong is proof enough for me that things have turned out way better than I could have imagined. All my selfish dreams and schemes, all my wishful thinking, and all my fearful imaginings would never have landed me where I am today, and I'm glad for that.

When I took that detour on the road less traveled, I wound up on a path I never knew existed for someone like me. Wow, what a trip so far! I can hardly wait to see what's next.

AFTERWORD

If I've managed to make sense in this little book, I hope you liked it. It's this layman's look at life. A lot of it tells some of my story to provide some context to my thoughts on the subject. I never thought I'd write a book like this, but for some reason, I felt compelled to do so. I'm going to call that a God thing because I don't think I could have done it on my own. I'm good at starting stuff but not always good at finishing it. It is not my purpose to tell anybody that they are wrong about what they think. I'm just offering my personal experience and point of view. Everyone can decide for themselves what to believe. If I've said anything that's true, I believe you'll know it in your heart.

Religion is a very touchy subject for many people. My aim is to hopefully lead nonbelieving people to consider that there really is a God and that the Bible is a reliable history book full of useful tools for living. It's not the easiest book to read, and it was written for and about an ancient audience. However, it is understandable if you take the time to read it along with other books that contain reliable explanations of what it's saying and who it's speaking to. I suddenly saw the overarching story of the whole Bible. Not just from Todd's book but from reading the Bible from beginning to end using the Bible Project (mentioned earlier) and consulting other sources mentioned in this book. Like I said, I always believed, *but now I know*. There is a difference.

God bless you all.

ABOUT THE AUTHOR

Sean Ferguson is retired and living with his wife and their two dogs in Hixson, Tennessee, a suburb of Chattanooga.

Having spent most of his working life in sales, he has one US patent for a valve design. He spent over twenty-five years selling in industries ranging from nuclear power, food, and beverage to refining and petrochemicals. He also spent fourteen years in telecom and wide area network sales. Ever restless, he even drove eighteen-wheelers from Southern California to Eastern Canada for almost three years in his early sixties. He says he still hasn't figured out what he wants to be when he grows up.

He's a former avid skydiver, motorcyclist, skier, and scuba diver. He enjoys traveling with his wife, reading, listening to music, and now writing.